The Secondary Teacher's Handbook

Also available from Continuum:

Sue Cowley: *Getting the Buggers to Behave*

Janet Kay: *Teaching Assistant's Handbook*

Lyn Overall and Margaret Sangster: *The Primary Teacher's Handbook*

Andrew Pollard: *Reflective Teaching*

Andrew Pollard: *Readings for Reflective Teaching*

Angela Thody, Barbara Gray and Derek Bowden: *Teacher's Survival Guide*

The Secondary Teacher's Handbook

Lyn Overall and Margaret Sangster

continuum
LONDON • NEW YORK

Continuum

The Tower Building
11 York Road
London SE1 7NX

370 Lexington Avenue
New York
NY 10017-6503

www.continuumbooks.com

© Lyn Overall and Margaret Sangster 2003

First published 2003

British Library Cataloguing-in-Publication Data
A catalogue record for this book is available from the British Library.

ISBN: 0–8264–5840–8 (hardback) 0–8264–5841–6 (paperback)

Typeset by C.K.M. Typesetting, Salisbury, Wiltshire
Printed and bound in Great Britain by MPG Books Ltd, Bodmin, Cornwall

Contents

List of headwords

Introduction

This book is about working on becoming a more effective teacher through a process of evaluation and action.

Outstanding teachers continuously set and meet ambitious targets for themselves and their pupils. They refer regularly to visible, quantifiable and tangible measures; and they focus on whether they and the school are making a difference and adding value to pupils.

(Hay McBer, 2000,1.3.9)

When effective teachers talk about how they work it is hard for them to express the complexity of decision making which occurs from minute to minute in managing a class. Success is a mixture of hard work, knowledge, personality, professional commitment and the implementation of a range of teaching skills. Professional knowledge and teaching skills are acquired and refined over many years. This book offers an analytical reflection on teaching strategies and a model for implementation of those strategies. From our experience of observing teachers and students at work, we feel that the self-evaluation process is one of the most effective ways to develop teaching skills.

Teaching is one of those professions in which it is difficult to feel you know enough to cope with everything that comes your way. There always appear to be new situations to deal with; a pupil who tests all your current strategies and patience; a new initiative to introduce, a new technology to assimilate. The feeling of 'I need to know more' never goes away throughout your career. In our ever-changing society, it would not be too extreme to say that we have come to accept an element of continuous development in most professional work.

As a student in training and a beginning teacher the learning curve is steep and initially driven by survival! Gradually the focus moves away from yourself to questions about school and college students' learning and the effectiveness of the strategies that you are using. Student teachers who learn most rapidly are those who reflect on their own development and take action to improve their teaching. You may identify areas which need development and set your own targets on which to work. The subject teachers whose classes you take and your mentors in the school will help you with this. This book is written to support that target setting.

In England a new initiative 'Teaching and Learning' (DfES, 2001) was launched by the government to enhance teachers' continuing professional development. There is an expectation that teachers will continue to develop their skills and qualifications and an indication that teachers will, in future, track their own professional development in a profile document. This already happens with newly qualified teachers (TTA, 1998). As a teacher you may choose to further develop your teaching strategies and will find the contents of this book a useful starting point.

Teachers are not the only adults who work with students in school. Often co-workers, for example learning assistants, are placed in charge of a group or work with individual pupils. They are faced with similar situations to the teacher. The strategies employed to deal with these situations will, on many occasions, be the same as those used by the teacher. Within these pages there are suggestions which will support the management of groups and individuals.

Within the book there is information on aspects of teaching, suggested teaching strategies and reference as to where you can obtain further information on topics. Additionally, to support student teachers in England, many entries are mapped to official documentation (DfEE/TTA, 2002).

Although the entries can be used purely as reference material, their main contribution will be as a practical support to developing teaching strategies in the classroom. Part One outlines how the teaching strategies can be developed as part of the process of self-evaluation. This is followed in Part Two by an A–Z of topics which promote the development of effective teaching strategies. Each entry has a first section to help you think about what is involved in the topic. Links are then made with other relevant topics in the book. This is followed by bullet pointed strategies for you to select as targets. An additional section offers further discussion on each topic. There are also some suggestions for further reading.

References

Department for Education and Skills (DfES) (2001) *Teaching and Learning*, London: DfES.

Department for Education and Skills/Teacher Training Agency (DfES/TTA) (2002) *Qualifying to Teach, Professional Standards for Qualified Teacher Status and Requirements for Initial Teacher Training*, London: TTA, publication no. TPU 0803/02-02 (weblink www.canteach.gov.uk).

Hay McBer (2000) *Research into Teacher Effectiveness: A Model of Teacher Effectiveness*, London: DfEE (weblink www.dfes.gov.uk/teachingreforms/leadership/mcber/).

Teacher Training Agency (TTA) (1998) *Career Entry Profile for Newly Qualified Teachers*, London: TTA.

Part One

The self-evaluation process

The self-evaluation process

We have observed over a period of years that the student teachers and teachers who make best use of the evaluation process make good progress in their effectiveness in their teaching. They work on how to manage a classroom and how to provide an effective learning environment for their school students. The process they use is similar to the assessment process that takes place with the school and college students they teach. It is accepted that assessment is a part of ensuring good progress for all learners. Teachers look at school students' work and comment on their progress against set criteria. This collection and evaluation of data are two steps in the assessment process. A third step is to act upon the results by planning an appropriate next step to take with the student. This process is known as formative assessment. It is an essential stage in the teaching cycle. It is not enough to say, 'I have planned this, I have taught this and that's my job done'.

Effective teachers respond to the needs of the students in their classes. They adapt and adjust work so that it builds on students' current knowledge. When discovering misconceptions, effective teachers backtrack and re-teach, so that students have correct understanding. Assessment allows teachers to recognize where students are in their learning and to respond accurately to students' needs. This can be described as a *cycle of teaching* which *spirals* forward as assessment informs the next planning,

– teaching – assessing (recording) – planning – teaching – assessing –

In this book we are suggesting that you apply a parallel cycle of self-evaluation and target-setting to your own teaching skills. By *closing the loop* on your own learning by assessing your needs and taking action, you can generate a model that carries the development of your teaching skills forward. You, or a mentor you are working with, identify a target for improvement. You then decide on a strategy to deal with the situation and try it out. Then, most importantly, you then need to assess whether your strategy was effective and can be used again, or whether you must try another. It is easy to see how this will enable you to build a repertoire of successful strategies for use in your work.

The process of self-evaluation

The process of self-evaluation has several steps. These lead you through the decision making that is required to solve a problem, meet a challenge or make a minor adjustment to your teaching. The steps are:

1. Identify the cause for your concern – name the issue.
2. Consider the available strategies.
3. Select a strategy.
4. Try it out.
5. Did it work?
6. If yes – keep it in the repertoire.
7. If no – select another strategy and try again.
8. Start at 1 for the next strategy.

1. Identify the cause for your concern – name the issue

If something is not going well in the classroom, laboratory, gym, workshop, computer suite, or wherever you teach, you will want to make improvements. If it is a problem, first you have to identify it – naming what you think it is. For example, you note that in your lesson:

some students are getting bored;
there is some poor behaviour;
some able students are disengaging from work and are under-performing.

This combination might have several causes but after some thought about this you decide that your planning and task for the lesson are fine, the problem is that the pace is slow. The slow pace is boring some students and giving rise to poor behaviour and less than satisfactory work. It could have been a combination of problems, but this time you decide it is one problem that gives rise to several 'symptoms' that you want to improve.

In this book, if you are sure you know what is causing the problem you can look up the cause directly. Sometimes you may have to read several sections and follow the links before you find comments that match the situation you are considering.

As the process of identifying the cause to be addressed and naming the issue may take some working out, it is often helpful to discuss the situation with an experienced teacher. They can often pinpoint the main cause and help you to consider appropriate strategies. If you are a student teacher this consultation procedure will be part of your training.

2. Consider the available strategies

Once you have identified the area in which you are working, you need to select a strategy. Some possible strategies are offered under each heading. You might feel that one or several of these are appropriate. Reading the commentary and reflecting on the issue could help you to formulate a strategy of your own.

3. Select a strategy

Select the strategy which you think will be most effective in your situation. You may wish to select more than one strategy and trial them simultaneously. Trying out a strategy might involve refining that strategy until it is effective. It might be that you set three targets to work at simultaneously. These may or may not be linked. A linked example would be that you have a student whose behaviour you wish to change and you have three strategies that you are going to try out. In the following example there are three strategies for dealing with a child who can be disruptive:

(i)   You are going to ignore interruption during the whole class sessions and deal with behaviour at the end.

(ii) You are going to ensure that the student starts on the task by sharing the first few minutes with him/her.

(iii) You are always going to finish any conversation with the student with a statement of praise about one positive aspect of his/her work or behaviour.

4. Try it out

Having decided what you are going to do, try it. You may decide to trial your chosen strategy over one or more days.

5. *Did it work?*

It is important to evaluate the effectiveness of what you chose to do. Sometimes the strategy you've chosen will take time to have an effect. Sometimes it becomes clear quite quickly that the strategy is not the right one for the context. Returning to ask whether it worked or not is part of the conscious process of permanently adopting the strategy or throwing it out.

6. *If yes – keep it in the repertoire*

If the strategy worked then give yourself a pat on the back and make sure you keep using it for as long as it is appropriate.

7. *If no – select another strategy and try again*

If success has eluded you, have a rethink and either persevere with the same strategy or select a new one. Not everything is going to work first time. It is worth talking to someone* about the situation if the strategy does not work. He/she might have a different view on the cause and can help you think it through. It might be that you have selected an appropriate strategy but it is going to take time to work. Some students can be resistant for a very long time: weeks, months or the whole school year! You might decide that a different strategy is more appropriate now that you have thought and observed more about the situation.

8. *On to the next strategy*

If you have been successful you will be ready to work on another problem, challenge, or minor adjustment in your teaching, so move on to your next target. It is important to sustain the momentum and make the evaluative process part of your normal practice.

A format to support the self-evaluation process

Example 1 shows a suggested format that allows for three 'visits' to the self-evaluation process. It is followed by Example 2, showing two examples of how it can be used in conjunction with this book. Example 1 is drawn from a need identified by a student teacher from his/her classroom experience. Example 2 is from a teacher seeking to improve an aspect of his/her work.

---

* Be selective, consult a colleague who will be prepared and able to assist your thinking.

Self-evaluation of teaching strategies	
The aspect of teaching or learning I wish to improve	
Strategy to try	**Evaluation**
	Success/try another strategy
The aspect of teaching or learning I wish to improve	
Strategy to try	**Evaluation**
	Success/try another strategy
The aspect of teaching or learning I wish to improve:	
Strategy to try	**Evaluation**
	Success/try another strategy

Figure 1 Format to support the self-evaluation process

EXAMPLE 1: MARIE'S TRANSITIONS

Marie, a student teacher, realizes that she is having difficulty moving the class from one place to another. One of the times is when they all finish one activity and have to move to the next, such as moving from a demonstration to the whole class, to follow-up activities and tasks. The students are noisy, start to wander around and some find other things to do. She usually ends up raising her voice, stopping everyone and telling them off. She also notes that difficulties happen when students finish their work at different times. These periods are known as 'transitions'.

Having identified where the problem lies she looks in the A–Z section of Part Two for 'Transitions'. Here she finds that there are several types of transition and several possible causes for them not going smoothly. At this point she needs to select what she is going to work on first. Is it going to be: clearer instructions; a different strategy for getting students to move from one place to another; or a change in the work set? She may wish to take on more than one strategy. The important point is for Marie to identify what is causing the problem. She may be able to discuss this with the subject teacher who may have been observing her lesson.

Having selected the strategy to try out Marie then needs to write it on the form.

Self-evaluation of teaching strategies

The aspect of teaching or learning I wish to improve

Transitions

Strategy to try	Evaluation
Clearer end of task instructions.	
Directing groups one at a time to tasks set.	
	Success/try another strategy

At this stage only 'The aspect I wish to improve' and the 'Strategy to try' sections are completed. At the end of the day Marie returns to the form to do her evaluation and consider her next target.

Self-evaluation of teaching strategies

The aspect of teaching or learning I wish to improve

Transitions

Strategy to try	Evaluation
Clearer end of task instructions.	*I still need to work on this.*
Directing groups one at a time to tasks set.	*This was much better, I shall keep this.*
	Success/try another strategy

The aspect of teaching or learning I wish to improve
Continue with transitions.

Strategy to try	Evaluation
Clearer end of task instructions with direction of exactly what each group is to do first and when they finish.	
	Success/try another strategy

From the way Marie fills in the evaluation we can see she has had some partial success but wishes to change one of her strategies slightly and focus again on it. She will maintain the successful strategy of instructing one group at a time.

EXAMPLE 2: PETER'S MARKING STRATEGIES

Peter, a geography teacher in his second year of teaching, has noticed that many of his students in Year 7 and 8, pay little attention to the marks he gives. Currently he operates a system where students receive a mark out of 10 for each piece of work. He collects these marks in a record book and averages them out for the half-term. He occasionally writes a brief phrase such as 'good work', 'satisfactory' or 'see me' on their work, as well as correcting errors in English language and spelling. He would like his students to show more concern about improving poor responses as well as correcting grammatical errors.

On reflection and having read the sections in this book on marking and feedback he feels he has two choices: to instigate a more complex marking system; or to involve the students in reviewing and evaluating their own work. He is not sure whether these two strategies are mutually exclusive, but opts to try and promote the second strategy.

Peter decides to begin the next lesson with students in Year 7 discussing with each other any mistakes they made. He is aware he might have to pair those who got 10 out of 10 with those who had made many mistakes.

Self-evaluation of teaching strategies	
The aspect of teaching or learning I wish to improve *Student engagement in addressing errors in work.*	
Strategy to try *Time slot to discuss errors with peers.*	**Evaluation**
	Success/try another strategy

Peter found that the discussion was useful because the students fed back to him that they were now more aware about their use of English and why their statements about the geography were incorrect. This was a gain, but the start of the session was very ragged and too much session time was used up. Peter therefore decided to adjust his strategy to make it more structured. He was not sure whether this would increase or decrease understanding but was prepared to seek further feedback from students.

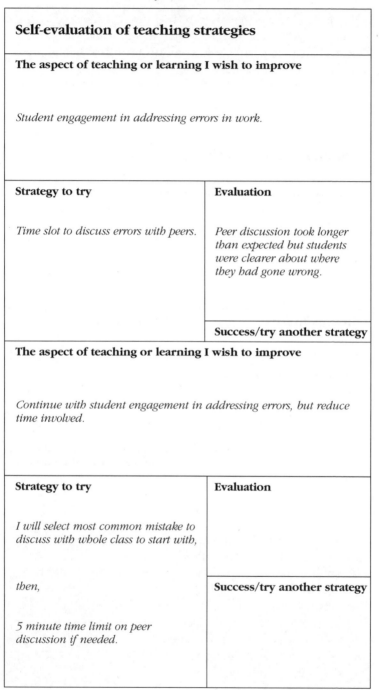

Self-evaluation of teaching strategies

The aspect of teaching or learning I wish to improve

Student engagement in addressing errors in work.

Strategy to try	Evaluation
Time slot to discuss errors with peers.	*Peer discussion took longer than expected but students were clearer about where they had gone wrong.*
	Success/try another strategy

The aspect of teaching or learning I wish to improve

Continue with student engagement in addressing errors, but reduce time involved.

Strategy to try	Evaluation
I will select most common mistake to discuss with whole class to start with,	
then,	**Success/try another strategy**
5 minute time limit on peer discussion if needed.	

Whilst the strategy Peter tried has led to more engagement by the students he has now gone on to question how meaningful giving marks out of 10 are and how constructive his comments on the work are to the students. He has begun to examine further his assessment and feedback strategies.

Further uses of evaluation strategies and target setting in teaching

In Part Two, the entries which are most directly about teaching include suggested strategies which are written in the present tense, in an instructional form. This is for use when carrying out the strategy in the classroom. For example, 'Allow 10 minutes for a plenary', 'Check the clock every 10 minutes to see if I am on schedule'. By changing the form to a question it can also be used as a check when planning. For example, 'Have I allowed time for a plenary?'. When evaluating the success of your strategy you will move into question mode again. For example, 'Did I allow time for the plenary? Did I check the clock?'.

Self-evaluation is a powerful process. Here we are recommending that you use it on your teaching skills. The same procedure can also be used in evaluating the effectiveness of a lesson. Did the lesson meet the objective? If yes, well done and move on. If no, then what shall I change next time?

It is also possible to use the process with individual students in your classes. For example, if you have a shy student you can consider what strategy you can use during the week to encourage him/her to join in group discussion. At the end of the week you can assess whether your strategy has been effective and decide on a new one if necessary. This could be recorded in the student's ongoing profile. As well as being a proactive way of working with students it also helps you to be consistent in your responses which sends clearer messages about behaviour in your classes.

International perspectives

This book is mostly about generic teaching skills. The strategies suggested will apply to many contexts. In countries where students training to be teachers are required to meet criteria or competencies or professional standards, entries can be 'mapped' against these. These could be integrated into the target-setting and recorded in the official profile. In England to qualify to teach, statutory requirements have to be met. (DfES/TTA, 2002) Where they apply we have mapped entries against these requirements. Some of the information-giving entries have general application, while others apply particularly to secondary education in England.

A note on terminology

Words mean different things in different countries. This book uses English terms. We write about our school-age learners, as students, pupils or children. In the USA and Canada, learners of all ages are students. In the USA, Canada and in some South American countries grades (classes) equate to chronological age but progression to the next grade is based on competence. In the rest of the world, children are usually grouped by chronological age and progress with advancing age. In England, most children enter schooling before they are 5, some start nursery education when they are 3. The 5-year-olds go into a reception class. At 6 they progress to a Year 1 class which normally equates to Grade 1 in most of the USA, and to Primary 2 in Scotland. In the UK, children are in primary school until the age of 11. These are known as elementary schools in Canada and the USA. Eleven to 18-year-olds in the UK go to secondary school, in North America, Australia and New Zealand these students attend high school.

In the UK education system, central government determines much of the structure and provision for education. For example, in England there is a National Curriculum with Key Stage tests at 7, 11 and 14. There are also national qualifications, usually by public examination, at end stages of secondary education. And there is a national inspection system. Wales, Scotland and Northern Ireland have their own systems.

In England, local government, in the form of local education authorities (LEAs), allocate funds from local and central taxation; however, funding is increasingly being channelled directly into schools. This has reduced the role of the local authority education department. Contrast this with North America, where diversity is considerable as education is a district and state responsibility. Some states have an outline curriculum and take part in some national examinations for older students, but it is not possible to generalize.

Terminology varies in internal matters too. For example, in English schools the senior manager is usually known as the head teacher, whilst in North America, the senior manager in school is known as the school principal. In the UK, the free time between lessons is known as breaks; whilst it is called recess in North America. School work in the UK is marked; in the USA it is graded.

References

Department for Education and Skills/Teacher Training Agency (DfES/TTA) (2002) *Qualifying to Teach, Professional Standards for Qualified Teacher Status Requirements for Initial Teacher Training*, London: TTA, publication no. TPU 0803/02-02 (weblink www.canteach.gov.uk).

Part Two

A–Z of effective teaching strategies

Able students

Often able students are talented in many aspects of school work. Occasionally a student has a talent in one specific area such as music, art or mathematics. Able students' cycle of learning has a different balance. Often there is a quick uptake of new learning, with the student making links to his/her prior experience. They need only a short consolidation or practice period and enjoy applying the learning to new and challenging situations. Problem solving is a good example of one way of meeting able students' needs.

Sometimes able students become withdrawn. Sometimes they get impatient with slower students and prefer to work on their own. As a teacher you have to find the balance between developing all aspects of the pupil, including working with others. You need to create opportunities which let the student stretch his/her abilities.

Some students are educationally advanced because they are more mature or, they have received rich educational experiences at home, or have been coached in a subject. It is the subject teacher's task to work out what each student is capable of and provide a suitably challenging curriculum.

Links

Differentiation
Expectations about students' learning
Group work
Problem solving

Strategies

- Increase an able student's decision-making opportunities.
- Lessen practice time and increase time spent on application of knowledge.
- Try presenting work initially as a problem.
- Adjust the group task so it is more challenging for the able student.
- Try to find times when able students work with you and with other able students.

Development

Much has been written about able students and gifted students. It is recognized that students can be talented at different things. Gardner

(1983) theorizes that multiple intelligences exist and the brain develops with strengths in a possible seven areas, such as spatial intelligence, music intelligence and numerical intelligence. It is generally recognized that Intelligence Quotient (IQ) tests are a rather general way of measuring ability and it is more effective to deal with specific abilities. This is not easy when teaching classes of 30. When trying to establish what able students know, it appears they can do all the things you ask of them within the normal range of the subject syllabus for the year group. It is probable that they can do half the work before you teach them so it is understandable that they get bored. It is vital that they engage in new learning. This may mean that you have to cater for their needs on an individual basis.

Alongside the academic needs of the able child, the teacher needs to ensure that social development and good working practices are addressed. It is very easy to isolate able students. They get impatient when working with students who think at a slower speed to them. They get fed up acting as a surrogate teacher. Other students can treat them as 'different' and find them threatening. They can easily get used to working on their own and some find it slow and tedious to articulate their thinking. A variety of approaches and experiences need to be utilized, appropriate to the expected outcomes of the task. Muijs and Reynolds (2001) offer a good account of the needs and organization of gifted students in the classroom.

Further reading

Gardner, H. (1983) *Frames of Mind: A Theory of Multiple Intelligences,* London: Heinemann.
Muijs, D. and Reynolds, D. (2001) *Effective Teaching: Evidence and Practice,* London: Paul Chapman.

TTA Standards

3.2.4, 3.3.4.

Active learning

How can we put students in a position to control their own learning? To be active learners they need to be able to:

  forecast how well they will do on various tasks;
  know what they already understand about the tasks;
  know what aspects of the tasks they can do.

Active learners can transfer what they know to new tasks. In a modern society active learning is important because individuals will need to be able to do new things as new challenges arise. Our responsibility is to enable learners to reflect on and improve their own abilities to learn. There are three main areas that underpin the thinking about active learning as follows.

Open formative assessment   Students come to our schools knowing many things. We have to know and use what each of them understands about our own specialist subject. This has implications for assessment. In the model of active learning it is not sufficient to test at end points. Assessment has to be a continuous monitoring of knowledge and understanding. Constructive and supportive feedback helps to make explicit to the individual what he/she knows and what still has to be learned. It is a way of modelling the process of reflective learning.

Teach less, more thoroughly   Exploring the issues about your subject, rather than trying to cover everything at a shallow level, is time well spent. This is not to deny the importance of completeness in any subject. Coverage of subject matter is important. This can be achieved by developing curriculum across the key stages and between schools.

In-depth understanding of subject concepts and factual knowledge is more important than superficial coverage of the whole discipline. You'll know which parts of your subject can be hard to grasp. To do this well you need knowledge about how students learn your subject. Your job is to make this learning possible. You'll do this by giving an overview, 'This is what we are learning'. Often you will break the learning into small steps and relate these steps back to the topic that the students are covering. A great many carefully chosen examples about one concept will help in this. Taking time to ensure that students' factual knowledge is accurate and secure is very important. End-point (often external) assessment should test students' deep understanding rather than their surface knowledge. This also ensures public accountability.

Taking time to ensure that students' factual knowledge is accurate and secure is very important. To do this your own understanding of factual knowledge and the concepts of the subjects you teach and their disciplines (ways of working and thinking) are crucial. Of equal importance is your knowledge about how students learn each subject. As a subject teacher both are prerequisites for the students in your classes to be active learners.

Teach learners how to learn The internal dialogue that goes on when anyone learns anything is important. Making this explicit to learners is really important. Recognize that your subject has its own *metacognition* (internal dialogue, the talk that goes on in the head). One way of modelling this is to let them talk about what they are learning. Working in pairs and small groups to solve particular problems is a powerful way of achieving this. You need to be able to help learners know how your subject works; you'll want to explore with them all the things that make it distinctive, for example, its language, concepts, theory, philosophy, processes and procedures.

Links

Feedback
Formative assessment
Independent learning
Recording individual progress
Self-assessment by pupils
Subject knowledge
Summative assessment
Thinking skills

Strategies

To enable active learning:

Before beginning a new topic:

- check what each student knows about the topic;
- know each student's preconceptions about the topic.

In your preparation ensure that you:

- are providing factually accurate knowledge;
- understand the facts and ideas within a conceptual framework;
- know which areas might be hard to learn;
- organize what you teach to make it easy to recall and use.

In each session:

- clearly define learning goals with the students;
- use small steps and really carefully chosen examples to make the 'hard to grasp' easy to learn;
- keep checking what has been understood;
- tell students what they have learnt about the topic;

- tell them what else they need to do to learn about the topic;
- tell students about the ways in which they have been successful as learners;
- give them something more to work on to be even more successful learners.

Development

Our understanding about active learning for students is based on a science of learning. Each of these headings provides its theoretical underpinning. They are starting places for developing a deeper understanding about active learning:

a. Memory and the structure of knowledge.
b. Problem solving and reasoning.
c. Early foundations of learning.
d. Regulatory processes that govern learning (including metacognition). This is about how the brain learns.
e. Symbolic thinking and culture and the learning community.

Further reading

Scott Baumann, A., Bloomfield, A. and Roughton, L. (Eds) (1997) *Becoming a Secondary Teacher*, London: Hodder & Stoughton Educational. Pages 351–5 provide some ideas on how to make learning active.

Capel, S., Leask, M. and Turner, T. (2001) *Learning to Teach in the Secondary School: A Companion to School Experience*, London: Routledge. Tony Turner's Chapter 5.2, provides a view about active learning.

Muijs, D. and Reynolds, D. (2001) *Effective Teaching: Evidence and Practice*, London: Paul Chapman. Chapter 8 explores the research behind some of these ideas.

Banks, F. and Shelton Mayes, A. (Eds) (2001) *Early Professional Development for Teachers*, London: Open University/David Fulton. Section 2 'Teaching for learning' has some useful chapters.

National Research Council (2000) *How People Learn*, Washington: National Academic Press. Seminal US report that used extensive review of available research to make statements about learning and teaching.

Sousa, D. A. (2001) *How the Brain Learns: A Classroom Teacher's Guide*, 2nd edn, Thousand Oaks: Corwin. A really practical guide on how to improve your teaching and students' learning through understanding how the brain works.

TTA Standards
1.2, 3.3.3.

Adolescence

Just by looking at students in secondary schools some aspects of adolescence are obvious and startling. For example, think about the physical differences between students similar in age and sex, some still look like children, whilst others are clearly young adults. In school, we are concerned with social, emotional and intellectual development of our students. Coleman and Hendry (1999) suggest that many youngsters cope well with growing up and that they deal with issues in their lives sensibly. They point out that the context in which this happens is important. Things like where your students live, their family, race, gender, culture and religion, will all make a difference to ways that they deal with the transitions they will go through. Different students will understand and deal with the stresses and issues that they face in different ways. The coping strategies that students have will be influenced by all sorts of things, including what happens at school. Teachers have an effect on the lives of their students. Often they can and do play a significant part in the changes that occur during adolescence. What goes on in school is important in adolescents' development.

Many, perhaps most, school students are not the stereotypical troubled and troublesome teenagers that appear in tv soaps and in journalists' stories. They cope well with the changes they go through. For many secondary students, their families support the development of self and identity really well. The family remains the secure base for the individual to develop. The evidence does not support the widely held belief that there will be high levels of conflict at home. Parenting style (see *Parents*) has an important influence on this aspect of development. Does what happens in school help or hinder the development of identity? For example, secondary teachers need to think about how issues of equity and autonomy are addressed in the classroom and in the curriculum.

Thinking and reasoning change during secondary schooling. Many students will enter the secondary phase thinking logically, but needing examples that are real (the concrete operational stage, in Piagetian terms). The question for secondary teachers is whether schooling enables the transition from concrete to formal thinking, from the practical to the abstract. Abstract thought shows when there is a greater capacity for logical and scientific reasoning. This is often demonstrated in the skills that young people develop and use in communication, negotiation and decision making. Does the curriculum help or hinder this development? In our teaching do we take account of the different ways that students of the same age think and reason? Planning for intellectual development should be across phase and across subjects. (See *Intellectual development, Linguistic development.*)

The physical developments of puberty have psychological effects. The radical alterations in size and shape, alterations in physical experiences and the rate at which these happen often cause anxiety. For many students these changes happen before they arrive in secondary school. It would be comforting for us to think that parents and teachers in primary schools have helped students to understand the changes, but we cannot make that assumption. Secondary teachers need to be able to recognize and help school students to deal with their genuine worries about the changes they are going through. (See *Physical development.*)

During adolescence, social development will include dealing with friendship, peer pressure, romance and intimacy. If we recognize that many secondary school students will be involved with sexual activity from early adolescence then the teaching of safe sex becomes important. It would be sensible to recognize that experimentation with legal (cigarettes and alcohol) and illegal drugs is also going on. These are concerns adults have about youngsters. Youngsters' concerns are not the same. They worry about appearance – weight, acne, what they eat and the exercise they take (see, for example, Shucksmith and Hendry, 1998). Getting on with others is seen as really important. You will recognize that these areas can and do affect feelings of well-being and competence. What teachers do to support social development, or to encourage emotional growth and good mental health, will have an impact for secondary school students. (See *Social development.*)

There may be important periods where some learning is most easily accomplished. If these milestones have been missed then schooling has to offer the opportunity for catching up. For example:

Motor skills, learning to walk, run and jump, may be best accomplished in the first six years. This is recognized in pre secondary education by giving young children the opportunity for physical activity.

Emotional control (see *Emotional development*) is best learned in the pre school years. It can be learned after the 'terrible twos' but may need more help right through the years at school.

Both first and additional language teaching from 0–12 years make best use of the capacity of the developing brain to acquire language. It certainly seems to be more difficult to become proficient in an additional language if teaching is delayed until 13. The implication for secondary education is that second language teaching should start with as little delay as possible.

All these, and other examples that you will come across, suggests that teachers have to take account of individual development to ensure that the teaching and learning are effective.

Links

Culture
Emotional development
Equal opportunities
Ethnicity
Intellectual development
Parents
Physical development
Social development
Values and ethos

Strategies

- Recognize that you are an influence on those who you teach.
- Build relationships with your students.
- Know about growth and development.

Further Reading

Coleman, J. C. and Hendry, L. B. (1999) *The Nature of Adolescence*, 3rd edn, London: Routledge.
Meece, J. L. (1997) *Child and Adolescent Development for Educators*, New York: McGraw Hill.
Shucksmith, J. and Hendry, L. (1998) *Health Issues and Adolescents: Growing Up and Speaking Out*, London: Routledge.

TTA Standard

2.4.

Assessment

Sce *Feedback*; *Formative assessment*; *Summative assessment*; *Self-assessment by students*.

Behaviour

See *Discipline*.

Bullying

It is useful to think of bullying or harassment as a particular type of aggressive behaviour. The bully intends to hurt the victim. The hurt can be physical or psychological, or both. When victims open up about this they emphasize the effects of bullying. There is no doubt that bullied students get extremely distressed. Bullying is generally thought to have three characteristics:

• It is unprovoked.
• It occurs repeatedly.
• The bully is stronger, or thought to be stronger, than the victim.

Bullying is repeated action; a one-off incident, whilst unpleasant, isn't bullying. More than once is enough to take serious action. Usually bullying takes the following forms:

physical aggression – being hit;
verbal aggression – name calling;
indirect – being ignored, left out, nasty looks.

Because of the consequences for both victim and bullies, it must always be taken seriously, this is not something that you can safely ignore.

Anyone, or any group, who finds that he/she/they can get a response by using aggression, can bully. It is difficult to detect, as bullying doesn't go on in the teacher's sight. Most bullying in school is well hidden and disguised. Often the bully will have a gang who support as bystanders, i.e. tacitly, if not actively. Most bullies will vehemently deny involvement in bullying. Whilst obvious victims are pupils who are different either physically, emotionally, or intellectually, unfortunately, if the circumstances are right, any student can be a victim. Also, any student can become a bully under certain circumstances. Bullied students may be very reluctant to tell, as often they think it is their own fault. Victims may blame themselves, they quickly loose self-confidence and self-esteem. They will find it difficult to concentrate. Some will take time off from school to avoid being bullied. Academically, they may achieve less well than predicted.

Links

Child protection
Communication with parents
Communication about learning
Discipline
Emotional development
Equal opportunities
Purposeful working atmosphere
Social development
Values and ethos

Strategies

This has to be dealt with through a whole school approach; parents and all the adults in the school and all the students need to be involved. It should be made a high priority. In the school:

- Everyone should know what bullying is and what to do if they encounter it, or if they find out that someone is being bullied.
- Monitoring of bullying should be going on. Anonymous questionnaires are an effective means of collecting this data.
- Breaks and school grounds need active supervision, with a range of activities to keep students happily engaged and a support network for students who experience bullying.
- Displaying helpline posters will help students who find it most difficult to tell.
- All students will be encouraged to take positive action against bullying.

In your teaching, prevention should be the key, teach how to:

- Build co-operative relationships with others through group activities and a variety of pairings.
- Resist bullying behaviour through role-play and peer discussion.
- Through role-play and modelling alternatives, deal with difficult situations without using bullying or violence.

Development

Bullying and harassment can be real barriers to learning. This is one very good reason to make sure that it is always taken seriously. Teachers need to encourage students to tell an adult if they are being bullied or if they know someone who is being bullied. This means that bullying has to be talked about regularly and frequently. Teachers need to be vigilant for signs of bullying; they should always investigate suspected incidents promptly. Parents need to be involved at an early stage. To achieve change, a problem-solving approach, working with both victim and bully to make the situation clear, can often work. Teachers need to follow up on all incidents to make sure that bullying is not resumed.

Further reading

Department for Education (DfE) (1994) *Bullying: Don't Suffer in Silence. An Anti Bullying Pack for Schools*, London: DfE.

Mosely, J. (1994) *Turn your School Around*, Cambridge: LDA.

Smith, P. K. and Sharp, S. (1993) *School Bullying: Insights and Perspectives*, London: Routledge.

The following webpages are useful on anti bullying:

www.antibullying.net/
www.bullying.co.uk/
www.scre.ac.uk/bully/index.html

TTA standard

3.3.14.

Challenge

See *Expectations about pupils' learning*.

Child protection

Child protection is to do with the role that the school has in keeping the child safe. In an educational setting, the 'child' will include anyone who is not legally an adult. A particular UK example is The Children Act, 1989. This came about through a growing awareness of child abuse and a determination to do something to protect children and young people. The key principles of the Act are:

- The child is a person and not an object of concern.
- Parents are entitled to be treated with greater respect and to be kept more fully informed.
- Statutory powers should be used only when necessary and last for the minimum time possible.
- Careful consideration should be given to the operation of inter-agency procedures.

In the statutory framework:

- The child's welfare is of 'paramount consideration'.
- Delay is likely to be prejudicial to the child and should be avoided.
- Courts should not make care orders unless it is clear that to do so would be better for the child than not doing so.
- Decisions should be made in partnership with the child and his/ her parents or carers wherever possible.
- Children have a right to be consulted and listened to when decisions are being made about their lives.

Both the principles and the law are similar in other countries. As in England and Wales, in many other countries the education service is part of the inter-agency approach. This means that teachers act not as individuals but as part of a shared approach. Teachers are not qualified nor authorized to sort out child abuse. But they need to recognize and report suspected abuse. In England and Wales teachers report to the named person within the school (every school has a designated senior member of staff, often the headteacher). This person receives training for the role.

Categories of abuse/identification

A child is considered to be abused or at risk of abuse by parents or other carers when the basic needs of the child are not being met through avoidable acts either of commission or omission. This means that a parent may be doing something horrid to the child or may be neglecting to do something, for example, providing regular food. Developmental milestones are important knowledge for you. You should know the physical and mental stages that children and adolescents go through.

Physical injury

Remember that parenting is very hard work and that all parents walk to the edge of a metaphorical cliff at some stage. Be open-minded, but be vigilant. Not everything is wickedness, but not everything is innocent either.

For example, consider:

- Black eyes – one occasionally is an accident, two may be non-accidental injury. Yes, we all know you get two black eyes if you walk into a lamp post.
- Bruising – fists make particular bruising patterns, so does the buckle on a belt.
- Round burns anywhere indicate cigarette burns and without doubt something that should be further investigated.

Neglect/failure to thrive

- For example, consider a school student who loses a great deal of weight during a school holiday.

Emotional abuse

- For example, consider the student who is obsessively good in your class. He/she may be in a home environment of low warmth and high criticism and is afraid to get things wrong.

Sexual abuse

- For example, consider a teenager who behaves inappropriately with others in the class or 'comes on' to members of staff. It is really hard to make this judgement. Be grateful that there are staff in school who will take this responsibility – but only if you tell them about it.

It is important to get this into perspective by knowing that abuse is comparatively rare. In England, 32 children in every 10,000 (1994 figures) were considered to have been abused. It is possible to go through a working life and never come across an abused child.

Links

Bullying
Discipline
Emotional development
Intellectual development
Linguistic development
Physical development

Relationships with pupils
Social development
Working with other adults

Strategies

What do you do? What is your duty of care?

- Take responsibility to teach about abuse and other issues that are about safety, e.g. bullying.
- Help students to know when to tell an adult about a concern.
- In your teaching be an active listener, high on warmth, low on criticism – someone a student can talk to.
- Develop trust between you and those you teach.
- If you suspect non-accidental physical damage or any other form of abuse, don't panic. Respond promptly and professionally – know the codes of conduct and procedures for your school – be careful to apply them. Be aware that you cannot promise the young person not to tell. In incidents of abuse you may not offer confidentiality. It is better to take action that later has a reasonable explanation than to have a young person suffer.
- Don't make a drama out of a crisis. Act on a 'need to know' basis. Only tell the people who are responsible for taking further action.
- As soon as you can, WRITE DOWN time, place, people, context. If matters go to court you will need a written record of the actions you took.
- If things look as if they may go to law, don't be your own lawyer, use support services.

Further reading

Used with caution, the World Wide Web is a sensible way to further research this area, because it gives access to up-to-date information. Most teachers' professional organizations and unions have access to expert advice on all aspects of child protection and other child safety issues. For example, www.data.teachers.org.uk gets you to the National Union of Teachers' site.

DfEE Circular 10/95 *Protecting Children from Abuse: The Role of the Education Service*, www.dfee.gov.uk/circulars/10_95/summary.htm This sets out what to do in English schools. Other countries will have similar procedural instruments.

DfEE Circular 4/95 *Drugs Prevention and Schools*

www.baspcan.org.uk/child_protect.htm   A useful website with links to organizations worldwide with a concern for child safety.
www.dfee.gov.uk/circulars/4_95/summary.htm   This sets out what English schools are expected to do about illegal drugs and tobacco and solvent abuse.

TTA Standard
1.8.

Code of Practice

This is a brief summary of some aspects of the Special Educational Needs Code of Practice, as it applies to schools in England.

The definition of Special Educational Needs

Children (i.e. the person at any stage from birth to leaving school) with Special Educational Needs (SEN) have learning difficulties that need special provision, for example:

a. difficulties in learning, significantly greater than the majority of children at the same age; or
b. have a disability which prevents or hinders them from making use of educational facilities of a kind generally provided for children of the same age in schools within the area of the local educational authority.

(Section 312, Education Act, 1996)

There is provision under the 1996 Education Act for children who are not yet school age to have their needs recognized and met.

Further definitions of SEN come from the Children Act 1989, (Section 17(11)). These include children with disabilities such as, 'blind, deaf or dumb or suffers from mental disorder of any kind or is substantially and permanently handicapped by illness, injury or congenital deformity or such other disability as may be prescribed'.

Disabilities Discrimination Act, 1995 (Section 1(1)) adds children with disabilities that have a 'substantial or long term adverse effect ... on ... day-to-day activities' to the list of definitions.

The Code of Practice (CoP) sets out some principles

The CoP states that a child with SEN should have his/her needs met, normally in mainstream schools.

A child with SEN should have his/her views sought and taken into account. The parent's role in supporting the education of their child is recognized as vital.

A child with SEN should have access to a broad, balanced and relevant curriculum (for both the foundation stage, i.e. 3–5 years and National Curriculum, i.e. 5 years old and beyond).

Some of the success criteria in the CoP

The plan for each child identifies the ways that all a child's needs are met, taking account of cultural needs, management needs and the way resources are best used in schools, that SEN pupils are identified early, and that 'best practice' is exploited in the plan for each child. The child's wishes and the parent's views should be taken into account. The assessment of need is within prescribed time limits. Statements about each child are clear, detailed and time limited and that the monitoring is specified and annually reviewed. It is expected that if the parents and the child want him/her to be educated in a mainstream school, that this will happen. At the same time, the CoP recognizes that a very small number of children have conditions so severe as to make this impractical. Some specialist provision will remain.

Under the CoP, *parents* are expected to be actively involved in the decisions made about their child. Account has to be taken of their views, attitudes, emotional investment and differing perspectives about the process, the child, the people involved and the range of provision. The parents' needs have to be met in setting up meetings, when these are and where they are held should be convenient for them. They must be told when a SEN is first identified for their child. They must be kept informed throughout schooling and involved in decision making. They have duties and responsibilities as well.

Pupils have to be involved in decisions made about them. Account has to be taken about their age, maturity and capability when doing this. They must 'not be overburdened when they have insufficient experience knowledge and without additional support' (Children Act, 1989/Children with Disabilities, 1991 regulations). They are to be involved in both the Individual Educational Plans (IEP) made for them and in the assessment process. As they get towards the end of schooling they are expected to start to take a lead role in what they are going to do with the rest of their lives.

In early years settings (i.e. before school at age 5 years) there is an emphasis on early identification of need. The adoption of a 'graduated approach' is expected. Early Years' Action (EYA) includes this cycle:

identifying the need;
doing what seems best to meet that need;
assessing progress;
stopping when the need is successfully met.

If it is not, EYA continues going through the cycle again, trying different approaches. If the child is not making adequate progress under EYA, this triggers outside advice and support: Early Years' Action Plus (EYA+) with, for under 5s, informal assessment every 6 months and, at age 5, detailed information to parents to inform transfer decisions. If the child is in school the Special Needs Co-ordinator (SENCO, see below) takes these actions. In other settings it will be someone with day-to-day contact with the child.

Schools (from 5 years to the end of formal education) use information that already exists with a focus of 'can do' and 'needs to learn'. In the primary school this action will use baseline assessment and other tests to make judgements about need. In secondary school, information from the primary school should be used to help inform action. During schooling, the teachers will use ongoing observations, assessment and feedback in planning to meet needs. Joint home school learning approaches will be encouraged. Differentiation is assumed to be happening for *all* the children in school. In the School Action (SA) phase a 'graduated approach' continues in the way outlined for EYA (see above). If the child is not making sufficient progress, then the school will move to School Action Plus (SA+). SA+ may include the writing of an Individual Education Plan (IEP) where differentiation is over and above what would normally be expected. The advice of specialists and resources from beyond the school may be used. Parents and pupil involvement remains active.

The CoP has provision to include early or interim reports sent for *children at risk of serious disaffection or exclusion.* These children can be dealt with under SA and SA+.

English as an additional language is not equated with SEN although it is recognized as requiring extra resources.

The curriculum for SEN children must use work from earlier Key Stages to allow pupils to demonstrate progress and attainment.

Local Education Authorities are to have a common style in all schools for EYA/SA and EYA+/SA+. *Each child with SEN has an annual review.* This is done within the school. LEAs are responsible for reminding schools which children should be reviewed each term. In Year 9, a link is made with Connexions for all students (a multi-agency service for young people, see *Connexions*). As with all students, this is to help the student with SEN to make decisions about what to do at the end of school years. *Connexions* will add information to the annual review. By Year 11 the annual review will have much more involvement of agencies beyond the school. The review must be sent by the school to the LEA within 10 working days.

The Special Educational Needs Co-ordinator (SENCO) has a significant role in all this. It is strategic, determining policy and whole school approaches to teaching and learning for children with SEN. It requires significant time to fulfil the role. In a school with many children with barriers to learning, it may leave time for no other duties. It has status, the SENCO is a senior manager with a special role in communication with colleagues, parents and pupils, and with those beyond the school. Part of the CoP is concerned with training and improving skills for both the SENCO and all those working with children with SEN. In some secondary schools the SENCO will manage a large department with teachers and learning assistants and hold resources for children with SEN.

Some children, even after SA and SA+, still don't make much progress. For these pupils the SENCO, in consultation with colleagues, or parents and the child, or an outside agency will start the *statutory assessment* process. Significant cause for concern will only trigger a request for statutory assessment when outcomes of EYA/SA and EYA+/SA+ are demonstrated. There will be many children in EYA/SA and EYA+/SA+, but comparatively few will require statutory assessment. This is the point at which LEA decisions become important. Children whose needs are assessed will not automatically be granted a statement. The school, parents and child may be asked to go back to EYA+/SA+, with perhaps more support. Statements, once written, generate additional LEA support and use centrally held resources (i.e. specialist staff). There has to be a prompt and flexible response to newly identified needs. The *statement* must be a precise description of provision for the child with SEN. Some children have needs identified at a very early age. They have statements before they start formal education.

In the CoP it is expected that LEA and schools will work in partnership. They are expected to use their best endeavours to meet needs, to find cost effective solutions, to provide information about mainstream provision for parents, to enable assessment to add knowledge about the child with SEN and to ensure that mainstream education is the norm.

Links

Connexions
Special Educational Needs

Further reading

Department for Education and Skills (DfES) (2001) *Special Educational Needs: Code of Practice*, London: DfES (581/2001). This document has all the details not included in the summary above. It is well worth reading the sections that apply to the age range you teach.

TTA Standard

2.6.

Communicating clearly

Communicating clearly is an essential skill for the teacher. This involves what you have to say and how you say it. Talking to large groups is not a skill we use in everyday life so it has to be learned. First, when planning to talk to the whole class, or the whole year group, or the whole school, consider carefully the points you wish to convey. If necessary, jot key words and phrases down on a lesson plan or small card. This will enable you to be succinct and talk to your audience rather than read to them.

During a lesson a teacher uses different voices rather like an actor. To gain attention your voice needs to be loud and firm. It is best to keep the attention gaining short, loud enough to be heard by all, and to use a familiar instruction such as 'Stop what you are doing, and look this way'. When attention is gained you can switch to a style appropriate to what you have to say. This might be an instructional style or a conversational style, but it will be quieter so that the students have to listen and will not feel that they can both talk to their friends and listen to you!

Whilst the students are working, you will be moving round the room or working with a group and your voice will be much quieter. Occasionally you will scan the room and may use short commands or name students whose attention you want to attract. This indicates to the whole class that you are aware of them all, even though you are engaged directly with only a few. With younger students sometimes you can praise someone in a loud voice which others can hear. This can make the student feel good and others want to work harder so that they can be praised too. This may be less effective with more mature students. With them quiet praise and extra challenge are often effective. Nevertheless, if most 'loud' comments, i.e. those you mean to be heard, in the lesson are either instructional or positive a better classroom atmosphere is created.

Expression and variation in your voice is important. All of us like to listen to actors and story-tellers. Teachers need to be a little bit of an actor and story-teller to motivate and convey enthusiasm for topics. Learn to use different tones to convey your expectations. After all, you cannot really get cross every time students do something silly, but you can sound cross so that they know they have crossed the line of acceptability.

Non-verbal communication in the classroom can be very effective. As you are talking to one student, the hard look at another, may be all that is required to redirect effort to the work set. Gestures, such as hand signals for rules, like chair legs on the floor, and reminders of safety rules in workshops and outdoor settings are important. You need to convey a serious interest in the work that you want your students to do. The way you dress, your facial expression and mannerisms are part of this.

Links

Behaviour
Communication about learning
Discipline
Instruction
Purposeful working atmosphere
Whole class teaching

Strategies

Use strategies to maintain a 'positive' atmosphere.

- Work out what you will say to the whole class.
- Plan using phrases rather than whole sentences, so that you can talk rather than read.
- Have a set phrase that gains attention and gives instruction, so that the students have no choice but to pay attention.
- Make inputs interesting by using a variety of tones of voice.
- Keep instructions short and clear.
- Use the tone of your voice to indicate your approval or disapproval.
- Be clear with younger students in what you say and how you say it.
- Use words and phrases to the whole class to establish 'presence'.
- Pay attention to your appearance, dress appropriately.
- Be aware of your mannerisms, reduce the ones that indicate stress.
- Use facial expressions to encourage and repress behaviours, smiles and frowns, used appropriately, will work for you.

Development

Teachers have different views on how to communicate with children. Wells (1996) summarizes a study on young children's meaning, making important conclusions on how teachers facilitate high quality conversation and guide children to reinvent knowledge. He contrasts these situations with a traditional transmission style of teaching where the teacher imparts the knowledge and the children are expected to listen and learn. These conclusions can be transferred to the secondary classroom where you need to consider the effects of teaching style on students' learning.

Communication can be more than oral comment. Cruickshank *et al.* (1979) surveyed students with the research question 'Clear teaching, what is it?'. The results were summarized into the following eight responses:

1. Gives us a chance to think about what's being taught.
2. Explains something and then stops so we can think about it.
3. Shows us how to remember things.
4. Gives us enough time for practice.
5. Teaches at a pace appropriate to the topic and pupils.
6. Takes time when explaining.

7. Answers pupils' questions.
8. Stresses difficult points.

Further reading

Capel, S., Strangwick, R. and Whitehead, M. (2001) 'Unit 3.1 Communicating with pupils' in Capel, S., Leask, M. and Turner, T. (Eds) *Learning to Teach in Secondary Schools*, 3rd edn, London: Routledge, has more to say about this.
Cruickshank, D., Kennedy, J., Bush, A. and Myers, B. (1979) 'Clear teaching – what is it?', *British Journal of Teacher Education*, 5: 1, 27–33.
Wells, G. (1996) 'Conversation and the reinvention of knowledge' in Pollard, A. *Readings for Reflective Teaching in the Primary School*, London: Cassell.

TTA Standard

3.2.7.

Communication about learning

If students are to learn actively then your feedback on how they're doing is extremely important. If you are high on empathy and low on criticism, this creates an ethos that is nurturing and will enable each student to do well. Because of the number of students you teach each week, it is actually quite difficult to get to know each individual. You may know about progress in your subject, but not about their hopes and fears. This knowledge is easier to have about students for whom you are responsible, for example, your register group or tutor group. You will, over the year, get to know these students really well. Break time duties, and other 'informal' responsibilities, including extra curricular clubs and sport, are all important in getting to really know something about those whom you teach.

Links

Active learning
Communicating clearly
Culture
Differentiation
Expectations about pupils' learning
Feedback
Independent learning

Listening and responding
Motivation
Relationships with pupils
Self-assessment by pupils
Target setting
Values and ethos

Strategies

Make accurate assessments about:

- the learning process – how does the student learn?
- progress towards learning objectives – what the student is learning?

Ask the student:

- how he/she learns;
- about achievement.

Tell the student:

- how you think he/she learns;
- about the progress towards the learning objective that he/she is making;
- success in both the learning process and the learning objectives.

Set realistic targets for improving:

- the way the student learns;
- achievement;

Both written and verbal comments should start with the positive, 'you've worked hard', 'you've really grasped this', before setting targets.

Make communication two-way, ask:

- how do you feel you've got on?
- how did you do that?
- what do you think you need to do to improve?

Help the student to set realistic and achievable goals for him/herself – targets have to challenge, but they also have to be realistic and achievable.

Development

The focus is on the students' 'performance' in learning tasks. When they do well, it is about telling them that the work is good. When they do less well, rather than blaming the students, it is about improving their work. You will also comment on how they did the work. This places the emphasis on communicating about the process and products of learning. This approach is thought to increase motivation and to reduce the incidence of disaffection. The long-term aim is to make students increasingly able to identify for themselves when they have done well and when they could do better.

The strategies above are based on research about how learners think about success. Some students put success down to luck, some to ability and some to effort. The three explanations have different outcomes. They should lead to a differentiated feedback to those who you teach. For example, if success is down to ability then if I do better:

> it might be that I've been lucky; or it might be that I've worked harder.

Either way doing better, I may think, is beyond my control. My teachers can help with this by helping me to think strategically. The questions, 'how did you do that?' and 'what do you think you need to do to improve?' are particularly useful for learners like this.

Further reading

Capel, S. (2001) 'Unit 3.2 Motivating pupils' in Capel, S., Leask, M. and Turner, T. (Eds) *Learning to Teach in the Secondary School*, London: Routledge, is a useful place to start on the ideas of achievement motivation as a theory, a basis for thinking systematically about talking and listening to students.

Both the following readings are about the pastoral role that you might have with a group of students.

Jones, J. (2001) 'Beyond the subject curriculum: the form tutor's role' in Dillon, J. and Maguire, M. (Eds) *Becoming a Teacher: Issues in Secondary Teaching*, Buckingham: Open University, is a sound chapter on this role.

Earl, M. (2000) 'Pastoral care and the work of the pastoral tutor' in Beck, J. and Earl, M. (Eds) *Key Issues in Secondary Education*, London: Continuum.

TTA Standard
3.2.7.

Communication with parents

Parents, the people who care for the students you teach, have rights and responsibilities. Your respect for them is central to establishing and maintaining a working relationship.

Partnership with parents, in helping their students to become successful at school and beyond, can be achieved in many ways. In most secondary schools contact with parents relies on formal meetings. This means that the social, cultural, sporting and fundraising events that schools put on are hugely important in building relationships. The effort put into this aspect of schooling is important because it builds bridges and helps communication. However, it should always be remembered that the power relationships between teacher and parents mean that partnership is likely to be uneven, (for example, in school, it's you who holds the position of power – you're 'the teacher', but on home territory the parent is the main decision maker).

Links

Culture
Ethnicity
Homework
Parents
Special Educational Needs
Values and ethos

Strategies

- Build your reputation with parents and students as a trustworthy and reliable authority by being positive and helpful.
- Get yourself known to parents and get to know them by attending social, cultural, sporting and fundraising events.
- Preparation for meetings and written reports which need:
  - accurate information about progress the student is making;
  - knowing as much as you can about the student, both in your subject and beyond, their behaviour, talents, ambitions and difficulties.

Be:

- Approachable – in face-to-face meetings, smile and be pleasant; in written reports use a style that is accessible to your audience.
- A good listener to what is said and to what is meant – sometimes parents are less than direct about a worry they have.
- Responsive.
- Considerate and polite.
- Serious.
- Constructive.
- Both honest and tactful.
- Well presented – both in person and in what you write.

Development

The idea of partnership, of a shared interest, is a key to success in teacher/parent working relationships. Partnerships between parents and teachers may be at several levels. In some schools there is a real sharing of responsibility for pupils' progress. Parents will be well-informed about academic, social and other aspects of their child's progress in school. They'll be active in informing teachers about things at home that may influence learning in school. Other parents will also be well-informed but perhaps less confident, less concerned and less willing to share information with teachers. Some parents are happiest to leave decisions to the teachers. This does not mean that they are not concerned about their child's welfare, just that they see teachers as not requiring their input. Some parents, and these are a concern, are uninvolved, and seem very hard to reach. However, most teachers have very comfortable and useful contacts with parents. This is not necessarily a full partnership. One reason for this is that teachers are often wary that parental influence may become interference. This can also be true for parents who do not wish to reveal their home circumstances to teachers.

Further reading

Cowley, S. (1999) *Starting Teaching: How to Succeed and Survive*, London: Cassell. Chapter 11, 'Parents', deals with how to manage this aspect of your work.

Thody, A., Gray, B. and Bowden, D. (2000) *The Teacher's Survival Guide*, London: Continuum. Chapter 7, 'Significant others', is another guide on what and how to do this.

McLaughlin, T. H. (2000) 'Schools, parents and the community' in Beck, J. and Earl, M. (Eds) *Key Issues in Secondary Education*, London: Cassell, provides further insights into the issues.

TTA Standards

1.4, 3.2.7.

Competition

Competition is part of our society and education system (exams, grades, sports). Competition need not exclude intrinsic reward but you need to be clear about its place in the culture of your teaching.

'Competition is good for you' and 'The World is a competitive place', are two frequently heard slogans. As with all enduring slogans there is probably some truth in them. If you are able to compete, competition can be enjoyable. If you have a chance of winning, it is a highly motivating activity. It does not take long for school students to work out what their individual or team chances are. Then, either they will continue to compete because they conform to what is expected of them or they become completely de-motivated and cease to take part. If they do not join in this can be infuriating for other team members and sometimes peer pressure is successfully brought to bear.

With these thoughts in mind, you need to think carefully about the competition you offer your classes. Many younger students seek to achieve house points, stars, teacher's approval, all of which are forms of reward. Students themselves often turn some of these into competitive situations. For example, 'I've got two house points, you haven't got any'. As the teacher, if you create a competitive situation, will success be accessible to all the competitors? Are there situations where reward is intrinsic? This means students are participating because they want to and they care about the quality of the product, or they see there is a purposeful objective. If there are no rewards on offer will the students engage/behave? You and younger students need to be clear about these procedures so that they can learn about their own motivations.

Older students may become blasé about reward systems. They need to reflect on the motivational influences on their own lives and learning. They will begin to respond to the world beyond school. They will see this in different ways depending on whether they feel they are able to compete and what rewards it will bring.

Success at school and in examinations, as well as social influences, will all be strong factors in this decision making. Debating this issue with those you teach is important. You'll want your students to understand what motivates them; to understand the extent to which competition is a driving factor for them.

Links
Active learning
Bullying
Discipline
Independent learning
Motivation
Rewards
Standardized tests
Summative assessment

Strategies
- Is it appropriate to make this activity competitive?
- Can all the students participating see that they can have some form of success?
- Is the reward suitable?
- Are the rules clear to all participants?
- How are you developing intrinsic motivation?
- Discuss with students the purposes and consequences of competition and when it is appropriate to compete or co-operate.

Development
Every teacher wants the students they teach to be well motivated and most teachers spend time looking for something that will motivate even the most reluctant learner. Competition is a powerful motivator but it does not work for everyone. One can consider competing against others or oneself. The choice to participate or not lies with the student, whatever pressure is brought to bear, be it punishment or reward. For the teacher it is a delicate mix between preparing students for an education system which predominantly measures success by examination achievements and developing a desire within students to do tasks because they are innately interesting or beneficial.

Muijs and Reynolds (2001) describe work carried out by Borich (1996) in which he describes three types of classroom, the competitive, the co-operative and the individualistic. In the competitive classroom the standards are set by the teacher, pupils give right or wrong responses, as judged by the teacher, and pupils have a sense of success or failure set against the achievement or non-achievement of these targets. In contrast the individualistic classroom encourages more independent decision making, targets are set by the students themselves and the teacher operates more in a guidance mode. Incidentally, in general, boys prefer the competitive classroom.

Wilson (2000) debates these ideologies. He concludes that we should work with students to enable them to clarify their thinking about competition.

Further reading

Borich, G. (1996) *Effective Teaching Methods*, 3rd edn, New York: Macmillan.

Muijs, D. and Reynolds, D. (2001) *Effective Teaching: Evidence and Practice*, London: Paul Chapman.

Wilson, J. (2000) *Key Issues in Education and Teaching*, London: Cassell.

Completed work

Students should complete their work. If the work is important, it is important enough to complete. It is a good habit to learn to complete tasks. Some schools have this expectation written into their teaching and learning policy.

When a student is not completing work it might be because he or she is off task and more interested in something else going on in the classroom. It might be that:

- something is wrong at home or socially, stopping the student from concentrating;
- that the work is too hard, he/she cannot get started and therefore does not complete in the time given;
- he/she is a slow worker;
- he/she is poor at listening to instructions;
- you have set too much to do;
- the student does not see the purpose of the work set;
- you have set the same amount of work to students who have different abilities or different speeds of working.

Responding appropriately to a student with incomplete work depends on the cause. If you have set an unreasonable amount, then it seems tough to keep students in at breaks to finish it or ask them to complete it at home. On the other hand, if the student has been 'messing about' then action ought to be taken. First decide on the cause. Then decide on an appropriate action.

If you allow work to be completed at home, some students may take the opportunity to socialize in your lesson and choose to do the work at home when they are on their own. Giving 'finishing off' as homework is not recommended by the DfES (www.dfes.gov.uk).

Links

Differentiation
Homework
Independent learning
Listening and responding to pupils
Special Educational Needs

Strategies

- Set amounts which can reasonably be completed by individuals.
- Use shorter tasks and let students move on to the next step if there is time.
- Set out clearly, at the start, what you expect to be completed and remind them of this goal at regular intervals.
- Try and differentiate the amount given to match the ability of the student.
- Help poor starters to get going.
- Set quick finishers more complex and demanding tasks about the same topic.

Development

When students enter employment they will be expected to complete all tasks, therefore it is appropriate to develop this work habit. With more support and control to start with you should be able to make completion of work a high probability. As they go through secondary school, students can be asked to make judgements about how long they think they will take, how long they need to complete a task and eventually to organize parts of their own timetable with less rigorous supervision. This is part of the move towards developing independent learning and working skills. It is important to allow these decision making opportunities in appropriate situations. You never know, when they have a place of their own, even the DIY jobs may all get completed!

Connexions

In English secondary education Connexions is a new inter-agency approach which will have an impact on the inclusion agenda. Connexions is a single point of access for *all* 13–19-year-olds, to help to prepare them for the transition to work and adult life. Having one agency for school students to use, may make some aspects of the move to work or further education more straightforward.

Links
Code of Practice
Inclusion
Special Educational Needs

Further reading
See DfES webpages for the most up-to-date information about SEN and Connexions: www.connexions.gov.uk

Consolidation

Consolidation is allowing time and opportunity for learning to take place. Not many people have the ability to remember everything they are told first time round. Students need varying amounts of practice at a topic before it is secure in their minds. The advantage of revisiting work in slightly different contexts also allows students to see the commonalties in more abstract ideas and enables them to deepen their concepts. This, hopefully, will lead to them transferring the ideas to new, similar situations.

Links
Able students
Active learning
Differentiation

Lesson plan structure
Medium-term planning
Special Educational Needs

Strategies

- Allow time in medium- and short-term planning for students to revisit and explore new learning.
- Consider carefully whether consolidation for particular students needs to be in the same context or can it be a new context (in which will the best learning take place?).

Development

Consolidation serves two purposes. First, it allows students to experience similar learning in different contexts and therefore expands their understanding of the learning and how it might look in different guises. This may even facilitate the ability to recognize where old knowledge can be applied in new situations (transfer). Second, it allows for practice. Rather like the number of driving lessons you need to gain your driving licence, we all need different amounts of practice before we feel secure in a new skill. We also need to try out our driving skills on different roads and in different types of traffic. This is an analogy for placing learning in different contexts, so that students can exercise their acquired skills.

Continuing professional development (CPD)

Throughout your teaching career your professional development targets will be met in a variety of ways. Your opportunities for school funding are most likely to be met where your targets are closely aligned with those identified for school-wide improvement. Some, perhaps most, of what you need, will be acquired in your school and local area. You will work with experienced colleagues for example, to:

- manage your classes effectively;
- differentiate your teaching to include all students;
- develop the curriculum;
- meet targets for public accountability.

Beyond the school, provision for continuing professional development (CPD) may be met in a variety of ways. This will include membership of professional subject associations, including teacher unions, attending local courses run for groups of schools on particular aspects of teaching and training for delivery of aspects of curriculum. If you are ambitious and academically minded, education departments at your local university will offer post-graduate studies, including masters degrees and doctorates. These may have a subject, or an age phase, or special needs, or management focus. It's often possible to build your own course from units and modules of work that have a particular appeal to you and to spread the work over several years. In England, the DfES offers grants for aspects of CPD, including bursaries for those in their second and third years of teaching.

Links

Part One
Research and its uses
Teachers' employment and conditions

Strategies

- Have a clear set of targets for your professional development.
- Evaluate your progress towards targets against a realistic time scale.
- Identify what you think you need to learn:
  - if this aligns with the school improvement plan, take part in staff development provided;
  - if it is a personal professional development target, seek other ways of meeting this.

Development

These days it makes sense to have a career plan. In England the automatic annual pay rises can no longer be taken for granted. Teachers are subject to performance management procedures. These will monitor individual professional development. This means that thinking about where you want to be and what you want to be doing is strongly recommended. You may want to be the best teacher ever, or you may want to be a manager, or work to support particular groups of pupils or you may want to change to another career. Have a plan, even if you later find that you take a different route.

Further reading

These books will help you to think about teaching as a career.

Thody, A., Gray, B. and Bowden, D. (2000) *The Teacher's Survival Guide*, London: Continuum.

Cowley, S. (1999) *Starting Teaching, How to Succeed and Survive*, London: Continuum.

www.teachernet.gov.uk   A possible source of CPD funding.

TAA Standard

1.7.

Culture

Culture is determined by the set(s) of values and experiences and traditions that individuals and groups hold. Cultural groups may be determined for example by language, forms of dress, ethical and religious beliefs, diet and customs. As a teacher you will have a set of expectations about the students you teach. In part, this will result from your own cultural heritage and the traditions. Your awareness about other cultural groups will inform your teaching. Knowing about different cultures means that you can choose methods, resources and examples that will help your learners. It also helps to avoid misunderstandings. For example, you may think that a student who has misbehaved is being defiant because as you tell him/her off there in no eye contact. In some cultures students know that it is rude to look an adult in the eye, especially when you're displeased with them. The student you think defiant, may be using home rules to avert your displeasure.

Links

Communication with parents
English as an additional language
Equal opportunities
Ethnicity
Relationships with pupils
Resources
Social development
Values and ethos

Strategies

Find out about the culture of those who you teach:

- ask the students;
- talk to parents;
- use the expertise of school staff;
- find out about the community the school serves.

Respect cultural difference, take care:

- over the language you use;
- to choose teaching methods and resources that are appropriate for the cultural mix in your classes;
- that your stereotypes, useful as they are, may need to be re-examined from time to time.

Celebrate cultural richness (but avoid tokenism).

Development

This entry has over-simplified a complex subject. Culture is not a fixed entity. Individuals are influenced by a great many things. A social justice agenda would place much more emphasis on the nuances of difference and equality. In the UK in 2002, there is political debate about citizenship and what this is. Understanding culture, with associated ideas about tolerance, politics, conflict resolution and moral reasoning, will help to inform your opinion about this. The entry on *Equal opportunities* gives further guidance.

Most people have ideas about their own identity. English nationals who are teachers, on the whole, are middle class and white. Because of this a middle-class culture may be predominant in the schools where they teach. The community culture may be quite different. Where the community culture is different to their own background, sometimes teachers may have lower expectations about academic achievement. The students you teach and their parents have ideas about how you will behave and what to expect from you. These ideas come into school and may be challenging to deal with. Cultural differences can conflict and confuse, teachers having one set of expectations that are challenged by students and parents who come from different backgrounds.

Further reading

See the equal opportunities reading list.

On the web the British Council site is a helpful starting place for finding out about culture www.britcoun.org
Embassy sites are often helpful as well www.ukwebstart.com or www2.tagish.co.uk/links/embassy are both useful links
www.dfes.gov.uk/citzenship suggest a number of ways that culture can be addressed.

TAA Standards

1.1, 1.2, 2.4, 3.3.6.

Curriculum

What is taught in school is called the curriculum. Around the world, what is included and what is not included in the curriculum varies. Some developing countries struggle to ensure that their populations gain basic literacy. In other countries the curriculum is centrally determined and content rich. Whilst in others there is little or no central government guidance; each school district or individual school makes a determination about what is taught and assessed.

You may find considerable variation in the ways in which your subject is taught in different schools. This is because the organization of the curriculum is decided at school level. However, in publicly funded English schools, the subjects that are taught are the same for all students. This is a typical example of a centrally decided curriculum, with the content decided for teachers.

In England, from the age of 5 until the age of 14, all students are taught English, mathematics, science, geography, history, design and technology, information and communications technology, art, music, physical education and religious education. When they enter secondary education, at the age of 11, the subjects also include a modern foreign language and citizenship. After the age of 14 years the number of compulsory subjects is reduced, students can 'drop' history, geography, art and design and music. Be aware that in England proposed policy changes are likely to reduce the number of subjects taught in secondary schools.

The 14–19 curriculum allows for some variations in its approach to learning. Students may follow a traditional academic route in school and college. Some may take vocational or occupation subjects, which will include work-based learning.

In England, the National Curriculum is only part of a school's curriculum. It is also expected that students will use the core subjects of English, maths, science and ICT across the curriculum. In England and Wales, all students follow a Religious Education syllabus, usually locally agreed between various faith groups. Schools are expected to have a daily act of collective worship. Teachers take some responsibility for students' general welfare, health education, including sex and drugs education, and deal with more general issues outside the narrowly defined National Curriculum, such as sustainable development and environmental education. In England, all secondary schools are expected to include Key and Core Skills teaching across all subjects. (See www.standards.dfes.gov.uk under National Strategy for more on this.)

Links

Culture
Equal opportunities
Ethnicity
Long-term planning
Medium-term planning
National qualifications
Standardized tests
Summative assessment

Development

Establishing curricula is a controversial issue. On the one hand, a detailed syllabus ensures that every learner has an entitlement to a particular body of knowledge and skills. What that body of knowledge and skills should be is always going to be in debate. What controls are there on what goes in the curriculum? That rather depends on what you consider is the purpose of education and how you achieve that purpose. Society and groups within society have different expectations about education. There will always be religious, cultural and political tensions. One might ask what expectations parents and pupils have of education? For more about this see Wilson (2000) who debates the tensions involved in the various views about curricula.

Another aspect of the curriculum which is evolving is the balance between teaching and assessment. In England assessment has dramatically increased within the last few years. Whilst this puts pressure on teachers to deliver the prescribed curriculum, does it improve learning? Does the learning improve over a narrower range of topics? Is this appropriate? As you see, lots of questions for debate.

From a social perspective a lot more goes on in school than delivery of academic subjects. Some have termed this 'the hidden curriculum'. This covers all those social and life skills that pupils acquire by being with other pupils. For some, this is the main attraction of coming to school and matters far more to them than the formal learning.

The National Curriculum structure in England is divided into four key stages:

Key Stage 1 is for students aged 5–7, Years 1 and 2.
Key Stage 2 is for 7–11-year-olds, Years 3–6.
Key Stage 3 is for 12–14-year-olds, Years 7–9.
Key Stage 4 is for 14–16-year-olds, Years 10–11.

In England many children enter school nursery classes at the age of 3. They follow a foundation stage curriculum until they leave reception. This is Key Stage Foundation. The 16–19 curriculum can be called Key Stage 5.

Each subject in the English National Curriculum has a programme of study. This sets out what should be taught in each stage and each year group. The attainment targets and level descriptions are also set out on a subject by subject basis. There are eight levels for all subjects, except for citizenship. There is also a description for exceptional performance beyond level 8. Each level describes what students are able to do. At the end of each Key Stage there are national tests and teacher assessment.

Key Stage 1 levels are 1–3, with most students at age 7 expected to achieve level 2.
Key Stage 2 levels are 2–5, with most students at age 11 expected to achieve level 4.
Key Stage 3 levels are 3–7, with most students at age 14 expected to achieve level 5/6.

In England, most Key Stage 3 students are assessed at the age of 14 on National Curriculum tests in reading, writing (including handwriting), spelling, mathematics, mental arithmetic and science. They are assessed by teachers in all subjects. These tests and assessments take place in May each year. The results are published for each school so that comparisons can be made. Some adjustments to results are made, based on things such as entitlement to free school meals, which allows for schools to be compared.

At Key Stage 4 subjects are mainly assessed through national qualifications. Schools' results are reported on the number of grade C or better their students achieve at GCSE.

Further reading

Capel, S., Leask, M. and Turner, T. (2001) *Learning to Teach in Secondary Schools*, 3rd edn, London: Routledge. All three sections of Chapter 7 provide useful further information.

Gill, P. and Johnson, S. (2001) '14–19 education: broadening the curriculum' in Dillon, J. and Maguire, M. (Eds) *Becoming a Teacher: Issues in Secondary Teaching*, 3rd edn, Buckingham: Open University Press, pp. 273–83 offers a thoughtful critique.

Maguire, M., Dillon, J. and Close, G. (2001) 'Reforming teachers and their work' in Dillon, J. and Maguire, M. (Eds) *Becoming a Teacher: Issues in Secondary Teaching*, Buckingham: Open University Press, pp. 63–73 charts the background to the changes that have happened over several years.

Wilson, J. (2000) *Key Issues in Education and Teaching*, London: Cassell.

See the English National Curriculum documents for your own subject and the secondary sector on www.standards.dfes.gov.uk

TTA Standards

2.2, 2.3.

Demonstration by the teacher

Both demonstrating and explaining are highly skilled forms of teaching. Having established your learning outcome, what it is the students are going to learn, you'll need to break down the demonstration into carefully considered steps. It helps to rehearse before working in front of the class.

Showing your classes how to do something can be a highly effective teaching approach. Some procedures and skills are most effectively taught through demonstration. Examples include showing students how to layout written work and safe ways of carrying equipment. You need to teach students precisely how you want these things done. Then they need opportunity to practise the procedure or skill. You need to check that things are as they should be and correct as necessary. You'll probably need to remind them fairly frequently to start with. Eventually procedures and skills become automatic. However, remember that a procedure or skill learnt in one environment, or under one condition, will not necessarily transfer to new situations. For instance, safety rules learned in science will need to be demonstrated and taught again in craft lessons. This is concrete and holistic teaching. Students see what it is you do and they can replicate it.

Demonstration through telling and using examples to model thinking is another highly effective teaching approach. For example, in mathematics a teacher might get at a general statement through careful questions and appropriate examples. Or, in English and social science subjects, to create informed opinion, the teacher may argue out loud, putting forward various points of view and the reasons why some are more convincing than others. Examples need to be carefully considered; choose these with real thought as to how they match to your learning outcomes. Case studies worked through in pairs and groups, with students explaining the work and their thinking about it, can be very useful. The work often needs to be placed in a sequence of practice, review and then application to new situations.

Links

Active learning
Independent learning
Instruction
Learning styles
Safety
Structure lessons
Whole class teaching

Strategies

Before you start:

• Make sure that you have everything you need for the demonstration.

- Make sure you are absolutely accurate in the demonstration.
- Think carefully about pace; be slow enough to be clear, but not so slow that it is boring.
- Make sure you've thought about safety.
- Practise your demonstration – rehearse your questions, predict possible answers, think about what might go wrong and what you'll do to put things right.

In class:

- Move students so that everyone can clearly see what it is you are demonstrating.
- Tell them exactly what it is that is being demonstrated.
- Use carefully selected examples (and as many as you need to make the point).
- 'Think aloud', modelling the procedure, skill and thinking.
- Use carefully chosen questions.
- Listen and respond to answers.
- Have some poor examples for students to critique.
- Do some examples step by step.
- If you are demonstrating a way of thinking, make the 'laws' of your subject explicit.
- If you are demonstrating a way of thinking, use case studies to show how ideas are used in practice.
- Give opportunities to practise with your support.
- Teach students how to check for themselves.
- Be prepared to re-teach until everyone has understood and can do what is required.

Development

Much of your teaching will be demonstration so it is worth thinking about what makes it effective for the learner. Sousa (2001) reminds us that the brain responds positively to humour, movement, using all the senses – touch, smell, feel as well as listening. Humour for example, has physiological benefits in that it wakes the brain up and, used with care, it is an attention grabber. It helps to create a positive environment for learning and it helps people to remember.

Further reading

Capel, S., Leask, M. and Turner, T. (2001) *Learning to Teach in Secondary Schools*, 3rd edn, London: Routledge.

Cowley, S. (1999) *Starting Teaching: How to Succeed and Survive*, London: Cassell.

Sousa, D. A. (2001) *How the Brain Learns*, 2nd edn, Thousand Oaks: Corwin.

Differentiation

All groups of students have a range of ability and needs. As a student teacher or a new teacher to the school, collecting information about the needs and abilities of all the students in all the classes you are going to teach begins on preliminary visits. Through observation, questioning and listening to students, talking to the teachers and looking at records you should be able to acquire sufficient information to plan detailed schemes. At first you will plan work which you think is appropriate for a particular group of students, but as you get to know them and you observe their responses you will be able to plan the next piece of work so that it more closely matches what they need. This will probably involve modifying your medium-term planning as you go along. Remember, your planning needs to include consideration of gender, culture and race as well as academic performance.

You can differentiate your teaching in three ways:

1. by task;
2. by outcome;
3. by support.

Some tasks can be given to all the students and they will be able to respond and learn from them. The task allows them to respond at their own level, this is called differentiation by outcome. Other tasks will only benefit certain groups, therefore different tasks or variations of the original task are given to each group. This is called differentiation by task.

When you differentiate by support you will be responding to individual needs. This could involve helping individuals, but also adapting goals as you work with your students. For example, when you see that an able student has clearly understood the work set, you might reduce the practice task and set him/her a more challenging task where he/she has to apply the information. If another student is struggling you might simplify the task or give a task which underpins the one he/she is attempting.

By differentiating tasks you are trying to facilitate learning. By matching the task to students' ability you are enabling them to build on prior knowledge and move forward. If the task is well matched, the student will engage in the task and learn from doing it.

Links

Able children
Active learning
Formative assessment
Group work
Independent learning
Learning styles
Questioning
Special Educational Needs
Whole class teaching

Strategies

• Collect information about level of performance and past experience prior to medium-term planning.
• Select grouping appropriate to the learning objective. (If all the students cannot respond, differentiation needs to occur).
• Make minor adjustments to objectives if necessary as you work with the children. (This involves having thought about possible extensions and simplifications when planning the lesson.)

Development

Whilst everyone recognizes that students learn at different paces and there is a range of ability in every age group, there is little agreement as how best to cater for the range. This is probably because there is no solution which is entirely obvious. Some secondary schools run some mixed ability classes throughout the timetable particularly in the lower secondary age range, although there might be some 'setting' for certain subjects, such as mathematics. Some secondary schools set the students for the whole timetable and some keep these students in the same sets for all subjects (streaming). Even within mixed ability classes some grouping will probably take place.

There is a trend recently to do more whole class teaching. This does not mean that students' different needs go away, they are catered for in a different way, such as various levels of teachers'

Differentiation

questions and expectations of different students' outputs. In this situation the teacher needs to consider differentiation when tasks are set, whether the students work in groups or not.

There is evidence that placing learners in ability groups has an effect on learning and self-esteem. Brophy and Good (1970) found that there was a sequence of low self-esteem and low teacher expectation generated by grouping students in ability groups, which contributed to low performance. Boaler *et al.* (2000) have explored students' perceptions at secondary school level and raised some thoughtful issues well worth considering. This research was carried out with 13- and 14-year-olds moving from mixed ability to sets in mathematics. They found little evidence that students felt that they were in a better learning environment. The results indicated that the lower sets generated low student self-esteem and low expectation from teachers. This was poorly justified by a very small percentage of able children who coped with the speed of work in the top set. Teachers tended not to differentiate within lessons and a whole class teaching model dominated in set situations. Many students appeared to find the single pace difficult to respond to.

Further reading

Boaler, J. and Williams, D. (2001) 'Steaming setting and mixed ability teaching' in Dillon, J. and Maguire, M. (Eds) *Becoming a Teacher: Issues in Secondary Teaching*, 2nd edn, Buckingham: Open University Press, deals with the issues of ability grouping.

Boaler, J., Wiliam, D. and Brown, M. (2000) 'Students' experience of ability grouping – disaffection, polarisation and the construction of failure', *British Educational Research Journal*, 26: 5, 631–48.

Brophy, J. and Good, T. (1970) 'Teachers' communication of differential expectations for children's classroom performance: some behavioural data', *Journal of Educational Psychology*, 61, 365–74.

Harrison, C. (2001) 'Differentiation in theory and practice' in Dillon, J. and Maguire, M. (Eds) *Becoming a Teacher: Issues in Secondary Teaching*, 2nd edn, Buckingham: Open University Press, has a useful discussion about the issues.

Turner, T. (2001) 'Unit 4.1 Pupil grouping, progression and differentiation' in Capel, S., Leask, M. and Turner, T. *Learning to Teach in Secondary Schools*, 3rd edn, London: Routledge, has an account of differentiation.

TTA Standards

3.3.4, 3.3.6.

Discipline

Discipline is about the ways in which students behave towards each other and to their teachers and the ways that teachers, and other adults in school, behave towards students. Discipline helps students to behave acceptably and is intended to repress and redirect misbehaviour. Over time, the goal is to reduce the need for teacher intervention so that students learn to control themselves. The rules that will be implemented must take account of the needs of the whole learner, the needs for good order in the school and for society as a whole.

The school behaviour policy establishes what it is that teachers do about discipline. Establishing a common set of values is never going to be easy. The values held by school staff and implemented in the behaviour policy may conflict with those held by the parents and students. Teachers and the other adults may not agree with each other about the rules and how to implement them. Time and effort has to be found to work through to an agreed set of values to underpin the school behaviour policy. Schools that tackle this through involving the students, parents and the community often develop very successful policies. School becomes the place where the student is made aware of the similarities and differences between the values that occur at home, at school, in the street and at work.

Links

Bullying
Emotional development
Equal opportunities
Ethnicity
Inclusion
Relationships with pupils
Safety
Teaching in teams
Values and ethos
Working with other adults

Strategies

I will implement school rules fairly by:

• having high expectations for high standards of behaviour:

treating students politely by using their names and a pleasant but firm tone of voice;

through carefully teaching the rules e.g. with students new to the school, explaining that for you, the instruction 'wait' means, stop, look and listen, that 'turn-taking' means listening and responding, not everyone talking at once;

- taking account of age and experience of students;
- being aware of the needs of the students whom I teach:

  by knowing that not all students find conforming to the rules easy;

  by knowing who these students are and increasing the behaviour demands I make in small steps and rewarding even the smallest improvement;

  offering opportunities for developing autonomy and independence;
- knowing about cultural and ethnic expectations, treating these differences respectfully and using this knowledge to reward and punish appropriately;
- developing students' moral and social understanding:

  recognizing that the classroom is one place where social understanding can be developed by raising and dealing with issues e.g. moral dilemmas such as 'when is it right to tell?', through discussion and group work.

Development

Misbehaviour is behaviour considered to be inappropriate in the context in which it occurs. In school this will include:

aggression – both physical and verbal and including bullying;

immorality – lying, cheating stealing;

defiance;

class disruption – where students talk out of turn or hinder each other;

being off task – day dreaming, text messaging, the American expression is *goofing off.*

The last two, whilst minor in themselves, constitute the most frequent interruptions to teaching and learning. Many school behaviour policies put considerable emphasis on reducing disruptions and off-task behaviour through carefully managing the teaching and learning in classrooms. The first three may be addressed in a number of ways. For example, reducing opportunities for bullying by having 'befrienders', i.e., students trained to look after those who find breaks between sessions difficult. Form and register group teachers use techniques such as 'circle time' to work on developing a strong ethos in which students are empowered to, for example,

deal with issues of right and wrong;
decide what is and what is not acceptable behaviour;
discuss what working well means;
explore how to resist peer pressure;
address current moral issues.

Often this will be part of the school's personal social development and health curriculum.

Punishment for failing to keep to rules also has to be considered. Punishment has to be just and must not deny the student access to the curriculum. The really serious 'telling off', by you or a more senior teacher can be effective. The telling off has a number of steps, these may include:

Identification of the misdemeanour (what the student did, e.g., 'The rule in our school is that we treat each other well, in the corridor you hit John, that breaks our rule').
The consequences of the student's action in breaking the rules ('John was hit and that hurt him').
Getting the student to acknowledge that the rule was broken ('Did you know that Mrs Smith saw you hit John?'. Use other sources of evidence if you meet resistance.)
A set of actions for preventing repetition agreed with the student.

The loss of privilege can be effective. The point is to keep focused on what the student did, 'you are being punished for breaking our rule', not because 'you're bad'.

To be successful, the student must regard the punishment awarded as fair. A way must be offered to enable the student to learn to avoid repeating the offence.

Further reading

All the books below offer excellent introductions on how to achieve good order and discipline in school:

Cowie, H. and Wallace, P. (2000) *Peer Support in Action: From Bystanding to Standing By*, London: Sage.

Cowley, S. (2001) *Getting the Buggers to Behave*, London: Continuum.

Mosely, J. and Tew, M. (1999) *Quality Circle Time in the Secondary School*, London: David Fulton.

Rodgers, B. (2000 UK edition) *Behaviour Management: A Whole School Approach*, London: Paul Chapman.

Thody, A., Gray, B. and Bowden, D. (2000) *The Teacher's Survival Guide*, London: Continuum.

TTA Standards

1.1, 2.7, 3.2.4, 3.3.9.

Displays

Displays can be informative, rewarding or interactive. A teacher may decide to put up a display as a stimulus for a new topic. This raises the students' awareness of what is to come and gives them time to seek out contributions. Students, the same as adults, like to know the programme ahead of the event, especially if they are required to contribute. Students like to see their own work on display. This is rewarding and motivating for them. The purpose of interactive displays is to allow learning to take place through students taking some action prompted by the display. The students visit the site and manipulate the materials physically or mentally. This offers an opportunity for reinforcement of learning that has taken place in a lesson or an opportunity to extend learning on a topic therefore this type of display is particularly useful at either end of the ability range. Examples of such a display might be interpreting graphs, solving a problem, sorting statements about an issue or using a computer program. The advantages of the interactive display are that the teacher can be elsewhere and the students can work at their own pace.

All displays should be well presented. If there is sufficient paper, double mounting helps to show work at its best. Neat titles and labelling with vertical and horizontal alignment give a professional look. Sometimes a few items look better than a crowded board. Changes in texture and pattern on the background add variety and depth to the overall look.

Links

Competition
Learning styles
Purposeful working atmosphere

Strategies

- Use a variety of types of display, interactive, stimulus, quality completed work.
- In medium-term planning identify lessons which will generate display materials.
- In medium-term planning decide which topics could be supported by an interactive display.
- In medium-term planning identify the resources you need to acquire in time to find them.
- If a lesson is going to provide display material plan an appropriate student output.
- Over a term, ensure that each student has a piece of quality work displayed.
- Double mount work where appropriate.
- Plan the layout of the display, use pins to arrange it before stapling, gluing or blue-tacking.
- Label clearly so that visitors to your room understand what the display is about.
- Keep the display tidy.
- Involve students in planning, mounting and maintaining the displays.

Emotional development

Over time, children move from having others help them control their emotions, to being more able to do this for themselves. Some researchers suggest that emotional regulation goes on throughout our life-span (Thompson, 1991). Individuals vary hugely in the amount of self-regulation displayed. Think of the ease that some people you know can cry. Others seem unable to show any emotions. This is an aspect to consider when dealing with adolescents. It is closely linked to the development of self. Whilst early nurturing and differences in child care may make a substantial difference to emotional development, outside the home, friends and teachers are influences too. Your influence is in the way in which you deal with those you teach. Your respect for those you teach is important in their emotional development. You have the opportunity to model appropriate behaviours in the way you manage your discipline and organize your teaching. With your students, you will have opportunities, both in your subject and in a pastoral role, to recognize and discuss issues that have 'emotional' as well as intellectual content, for example, equity and equality, prejudice and fairness.

There are two areas of study that are associated with our understanding of emotion which help explain why students may react differently in classroom contexts. One is temperament: you'll know the sort of person that you are, for example you may 'be able to argue for England', or you might be easy going, taking everything in your stride. Your temperament is closely tied to your emotional type. The other is emotional type, which is partly determined through early experiences in the home, in particular the attachment between babies and parents. The extent to which temperament and emotional type is genetically determined is still not clear.

Being able to make judgements about another's feelings, the emotional state – on a continuum of happiness to sadness; the emotions of fear, anger, rage, guilt, shame, envy – develops from birth. Through childhood into early adolescence, an ability to understand how others feel becomes increasingly sophisticated. As the child's intellectual understanding develops, it seems that more than one emotion and the relationship between them becomes established, e.g. by 8 years old many children will say things like, 'I'm cross when I'm interrupted, but I'm happy to go out to play'.

Babies connect first with those who care for them. Adults are able to reinforce the expressions that their 6–8 week old babies make. Smiles are met with smiles; facial expressions are used to monitor the supposed emotion. This seems to be the beginning of developing a range of emotions. The baby's smiles are gradually given more readily to the adults who make most difference to him/her. Seven–nine months old babies show 'stranger distress' (Sroufe,1996); the emotions of fear and anger also develop at about this time. Much of the display of emotion seems to be part of intellectual growth. There seems no doubt that toddlers learn, from the reactions of others, a whole range of emotions and how to show these. For example, by age 2, infants will switch from pouting to crying if this is to their advantage.

Links

Adolescence
Intellectual development
Linguistic development
Parents
Physical development
Social development

Further reading

Coleman, J. C. and Hendry, L. B. (1999) *The Nature of Adolescence*, 3rd edn, London: Routledge.
Keenan, T. (2002) *An Introduction to Child Development*, London: Sage.
Meece, J. L. (1997) *Child and Adolescent Development for Educators*, New York: McGraw Hill.
Sroufe, L. A. (1996) *Emotional Development: The Organization of Emotional Life in the Early Years*, New York: Wiley.
Thompson, R. A. (1991) 'Emotional regulation and emotional development', *Educational Psychology Review*, 3, 269–307.

TAA Standards

1.2, 2.4.

English as an additional language

English as an additional language (EAL) is an everyday experience in many classrooms. In England, 'over half a million children do not have English as a first language' (DfEE,1997: 34). Every teacher is expected to promote EAL in their teaching. The question is, does spoken and written language and reading develop 'naturally' or does something have to be done about it in school? Often the natural approach works quite well, especially for very young children who may seem to learn easily and rapidly. After they are about 8 years old, some bilingual children seem not to progress as well as others. If we leave the learning of English to chance, it seems that there may be a barrier to achieving in school. Best advice seems to be for schools to have a specific policy, curriculum and staff with expertise for success in EAL.

Links

Culture
Equal opportunities

Ethnicity
Linguistic development

Strategies

First, establish some facts:

- What country and language(s)?
- Refugee or migrant?
- How much English is spoken at home?
- Are there other students or adults in school with the same language?

Then, do what you can to promote and maintain the student's first language:

- Find someone who speaks the student's language.
- Continue the learning in the student's own language as much and for as long as possible.
- Remember listening (getting the student to hear English) precedes talking, and speech precedes reading and writing.
- It is also worth reminding yourself that the conventions of English, where we read from left to right and the writing 'sits' on the line, may be very different to the student's own language.

Development

Many students who are learning EAL grow up to be fluent and literate in English. They may also speak their first language well but will not always be able to read or write it. If we insist that students only speak English we are making a statement about the value we place on homes and families. The student's heritage needs to be valued. The language of the home and the community need to be celebrated. Ideally, we might want to promote bilingualism or even, multilingualism. This means that whilst we expect the student to use English for communication both in spoken and written form, and to know about its rules, grammar and conventions; we would at the same time, be actively promoting the student's first and additional languages. This is a cross curricular, cross phase challenge. It's worth remembering that students with EAL offer a remarkable enrichment to the life of a school.

Further reading

Dillon, J. and Maguire, M. (Eds) (2001) *Becoming a Teacher: Issues in Secondary Teaching*, 2nd edn, Buckingham: Open University Press, Chapter 19 by Harris, R. and Leung, C., 'English as an additional language: challenges of identity in the multilingual and multiethnic classroom', is an excellent introduction to the issues that surround EAL.

DfEE (1997) *Excellence in Schools*, London: Stationery Office.

Mohan, B., Leung, C. and Davidson, C. (Eds) (2001) *English as a Second Language in the Mainstream: Teaching, Learning and Identity*, London: Longman.

TTA Standards

3.2.5, 3.3.5.

Equal opportunities

A useful place to start is to think about who we are and what contributes to our values. This list is not comprehensive, but think about:

your *gender* including sexual orientation;

what you look like, your *physical* appearance, including race, disability, age;

the sort of *family* you come from, nuclear, extended, single parent;

your *religion* and *culture*;

your ability to *communicate*, including your language, standard English dialect, Yorkshire dialect, English as an additional language;

where you live, inner city, suburbs, in the country;

and, perhaps most importantly, your *wealth* or *status*, i.e. middle income, low income, professional job, clerical job, unskilled job, unemployed, etc.

Some of these, maybe all of them, will contribute to your identity. Teaching is not a neutral activity so your values and who you are will have an effect on those whom you teach. Equal opportunities is about being inclusive in the way you deal with all your students. Treating them all in the same way will not serve. To be fair you have to meet the needs of individuals as far as you can. Students' attitudes to you and the school come from their home, their community and the teachers they have worked with at the primary stage. Often these might conflict with your norms. Your expectations and theirs may not match. Even their experience of things like the way you talk might be unfamiliar. When you ask once, at home they may be nagged. What you say as a joke may be misunderstood, regarded as offensive or even as racist. In your teaching, help all students to:

value themselves;
find similarities between their own lives and the lives of others;
learn from each other;
not feel that they are better than others because of their race, gender or wealth.

Links

Culture
English as an additional language
Ethnicity
Expectations about students' learning
Gender

Strategies

- Be conscious that your own attitudes are influential by, for example:
  making a real effort to get unfamiliar names correct;
  valuing the process of learning as well as the product;
  avoiding remarks that start, 'girls don't ...', 'boys don't ...';
  setting high expectations about success.
- Value student's home experience by, for example, gaining the knowledge that enables you to emphasize the similarities and positive aspects of different families' life at home.
- Deal with questions about gender, race, and disability, frankly and honestly.
- Take care over dealing with issues about homosexuality as these are subject to some legal restriction – take advice from your professional association/union.
- Deal with any racist name calling sensitively:
  support the victim;
  make reference to school policy;
  don't blow it out of proportion.

- See that adult to adult relationships in school provide positive role-models for students, for example, by distribution of roles to avoid gender bias.
- Your teaching is planned and delivered with equality of opportunity always considered. Plan to:
  use student's prior experience;
  use collaborative group work;
  ensure that girls, minority ethnic students and boys all get to take leading roles;
  differentiate tasks;
  allow for some same-sex paired work;
  allow for first language to be used in pair work;
  choose resources that are checked for bias, use positive images and are up-to-date.
- In predominantly white schools ensure that the curriculum reflects a multi-racial society.

Development

This is a complex area and one where it is easy to feel 'in the wrong'. At a personal level it often seems too hard to be fair to all the students in the class all the time. Some students do need more of your attention and time at particular points. If you feel this is happening too often, you should do something about it. One way is to consciously limit yourself to spending slightly less time with more demanding students and slightly more time with those who less often get your full attention.

Further reading

Hill, D. and Cole, M. (Eds) (1999) *Promoting Equality in Secondary Schools*, London: Cassell. One of the most comprehensive textbooks around this deals both with the theoretical background and the practical outcomes for teachers.

Mosely, J. and Tew, M. (1999) *Quality Circle Time in the Secondary School*, London: David Fulton. A practical book which provides sound ways of dealing with many sensitive issues.

There are very good sources on the WWW:

www.cre.gov.uk has useful links to many educational resources.

www.dfes.gov.uk is the place to look for up-to-date central government guidance.

TTA Standard

3.3.14.

Ethnicity

In the UK population of approximately 54 million about 6 per cent are from minority ethnic groups, (1991 census figures). Ballard and Kalra, (1994, p. 11) estimate that about 11 per cent of the school population are from minority ethnic groups. The drive from the UK government is to ensure that all students in our schools achieve high standards. In the past there is evidence that some groups, for example, both Afro-Caribbean students (Gillborn and Mirza, 2000) and white boys from working class background are doing less well in public examinations and national tests. Developing your understanding and having a positive attitude about students from different ethnic backgrounds, along with a commitment to their success is a requirement (Children Act, 1989) as well as a professional standard (DfES/TTA, 2002). As a teacher you will have a set of expectations about the students you teach. In part this will result from your own ethnicity. Your race, like your status in society and your gender, raises expectations in the students you teach about how you as a teacher/person will act. They will come to school with attitudes informed by their families' experience in the community. Home behaviour, child to child, adult to child, child to adult and adult to adult may be different from your own experience. Your awareness about ethnic groups other than your own will inform your teaching. Knowing about differences and similarities means that you can choose methods, resources and examples that will help your learners. It also helps to avoid misunderstandings and false expectations.

Links

Culture
Equal opportunities
Gender

Strategies

See strategies suggested for *Equal opportunities.*

Development

Cole (1997, p. 53) argues that in UK schools there are three approaches to education and that each is a strongly held position. The teachers in some schools have a monocultural attitude that 'attempts to make everyone "socially and culturally British" '. Others adopt a multicultural policy that celebrates cultural and religious difference. The last group of teachers adopts anti-racist policies that actively challenges all aspects of discrimination. Any of the above positions seem to place schooling as central in attitude forming. This would suggest that what teachers do about this issue is important.

Further reading

Ballard, R. and Kalra, V. S. (1994) *Ethnic Dimensions of the 1991 Census: A Preliminary Report*, Manchester: University of Manchester Census Group.

Cole, M. (1997) 'Equality and primary education: what are the conceptual issues?' in Cole, M., Hill, D. and Shan, S. (Eds) *Promoting Equality in Primary Schools*, London: Cassell, pp. 48–75.

Department for Education and Skills (2002) *Qualifying to Teach: Professional Standards for Qualified Teacher Status and Requirements for Initial Teacher Training* (TPU 0803/02-02), London: Teacher Training Agency.

Gillborn, D. and Mirza, H. S. (2000) *Educational Inequality: Mapping Race, Class and Gender: A Synthesis of Research Evidence*, London: OFSTED see website www.ofsted.gov.uk.

Hill, D. and Cole, M. (Eds) (1999) *Promoting Equality in Secondary Schools*, London: Cassell.

TTA Standards

3.1.2, 3.3.6.

Evaluating lessons (assessing the meeting of learning objectives)

Lessons are evaluated for several reasons. The main one is to ensure learning has taken place. You will need to assess whether the students have met the set objective(s). If they have this will inform you that the lesson was effective and will provide information for individual records. When learning has not taken place it is important to reflect on what has happened and make decisions about adjusting the approach. It might be that the objective was not appropriate for all or some of the students. Maybe it was too hard or too easy; in either case the students did not engage in the work. It might be that the planned activities did not match and support the objective. Possibly they learned something else or were confused. Maybe your teaching techniques still need to be developed so that a purposeful working atmosphere can be created. Maybe a combination of rehearsals for the school play and visit by the school photographer has completely disrupted the lesson. In this case, even the best teachers give in gracefully.

Once you have analysed the lesson you need to make decisions about how you will approach the next lesson. Your decision may be an action that might be appropriate for all your lessons or a strategy you plan to use with that particular group of students.

Links

Active learning
Formative assessment
Independent learning
Learning objectives
Medium-term planning
Summative assessment
Target setting

Strategies

A simple evaluation of the lesson might fall into the following categories:

Students   Noted individual student performance to records/who needs help.

Activity   Did the activities support the objectives well and would I use them again?

Teacher   What teacher skills did I use well/need to change?

Development

There are a lot of things which can go wrong with lessons. Even for the best teachers, lessons which go really well are not as common as people think. One aim is to ensure that all lessons are of a reasonable quality. With good preparation and a continuing proactive approach to improving your teaching skills this should come about.

It really is important to check that students have learned what you intended rather than something else or nothing. The standards you set them have to be high and you will want all your students to achieve well. Some students learn very slowly, others learn quickly; your lessons have to accommodate this. The misapprehensions and mistakes about topics are individual, each student's understanding is different and unique. Your understanding and reflection about these issues will help you to make decisions about what to teach next, what to repeat, what to extend and what new learning the particular group needs.

Part of your evaluation should include the students' comments on their learning. It is important to encourage and develop their self-evaluation skills too.

Further reading

Cowley, S. (1999) *Starting Teaching: How to Succeed and Survive*, London: Continuum.

Expectations about students' learning (challenge)

Challenge is about engaging students in thinking and working on the borders of their knowledge. Educational experience is a mixture of challenge, routine and review. Challenging students gives them the opportunity to take risks, to apply knowledge, to adopt new understanding, to work in context and to experience the thrill of being discoverers. This last is a highly motivating and engaging feeling.

Consider the thought that most of the adult world is about both routine and challenge. We do need to educate students to sustain the routine and to meet challenge and deal with both. Also, remember that all students can be challenged at their own level. It is not just a target for able students. It is about everyone who you teach.

Students like to know where they are so that they have some control in lessons. They also enjoy revisiting the familiar because it reaffirms their belief that there are things they can do and be successful at. Games, problems and computer programs in your lessons are good examples of useful contexts for revisiting situations. Students also like challenge where they are required to draw on their knowledge to resolve unfamiliar situations.

Teachers like to present a range of situations, too. There are the times when routine is strong and skills and knowledge are built in a formal way without having to set up new procedures, for example, in this category fall such things as sports training, skill building exercises, and journal writing. Then there are times when the teacher wants students to use the knowledge and skills they have acquired. This could be by asking students to bring their problem solving skills to new situations which will lead to new learning or a chance to apply knowledge to a problem in a context they have already worked on.

Links

Able students
Active learning
Curriculum
Differentiation
Independent learning
Motivation
Problem solving
Thinking skills

Strategies

- Provide a balance in your lessons and medium-term planning of the type of work provided; routine, new learning, review/ consolidation, challenge.
- Ensure students have the opportunity to apply their knowledge in new contexts.
- Differentiate work where possible.
- Have lots of problem solving!

Development

There is a considerable body of evidence building, from the time of Piaget through to present day research into thinking skills, that problem solving contributes to developing effective learning skills. Challenging a person's thinking is what forces them to adjust or confirm the views they already hold. Discussing how to solve problems means a person has to articulate their ideas and have others comment on them. This is a strong strategy for clarifying strategy. Maybe this is the territory where learning, which can be transferred to other new situations, takes place.

On a more individual note, it is worth reflecting on what our expectations are of particular students. Is it wise to form the view that:

He cannot possibly solve problems;
They are only capable of copying;

She can only manage book 4;
I need to work with this group of students because they are of low ability in language skills?

Our perceptions of students are clearly conveyed by our communications with them. If we have low expectations, students will believe that is all they are capable of. We need to be very careful about what we convey and expect.

TTA Standards
3.1.1, 3.2.4.

Expectations of students' behaviour

See *Discipline.*

Explaining

Teaching by explanation is an effective way of encouraging learning. You need to get on well with students for this to be successful. Poor explanation will be a source of frustration and tension in class. Careful preparation is a key to engaging students. Getting the right mixture of instruction, questioning and the pace of your whole class teaching is important. The lone or small number of students who need you to go over what you have just explained to the whole class will eat into your teaching time. Think about the additional explanation that these students will need and how you can plan this into the session. You may be able to use classroom assistants for this, or you may need to set the class going on activities and return to these students.

Links
Demonstration by the teacher
Instruction
Pace
Questioning
Whole class teaching
Working with other adults

Strategies

- Make sure that you understand what you are explaining.
- Teach new material as soon as you have students' attention in a lesson.
- Make good use of any additional adults to support students who are unclear about what they are to do or are slow starting tasks, or return to these students as soon as you have seen the tasks you've set are underway for most of the class.
- Take account of students' previous knowledge and experience of the topic.
- Link your explanation to students' knowledge, experience and interests.
- Use language that your students can understand.
- Tell students what it is that they are going to learn.
- Break your explanation into small steps.
- Use carefully chosen examples, as many as you need to get the point across.
- Allow time for practice and rehearsal.
- Review your explanation with students at the end of the lesson.

Development

Sousa's (2001) analysis of a forty-minute lesson suggests that the first twenty minutes is the best time to introduce new information. He suggests that you should avoid asking students about the topic in the introduction to your explanation. This is because if you get a wrong answer from students at this point, it will 'contaminate' the explanation. The next ten to fifteen minutes should be used to allow students to engage on activities related to the new topic. The last chunk of time gives you a chance to review the new knowledge the students have. This is one style of teaching. Another school of thought would recommend a less formal approach where explanation follows challenge, in the belief that students are more engaged in learning if they develop a need to know. This can also lead to opportunities for students to explain to their peers and the teacher how they have carried out tasks.

Further reading

Capel, S., Leask, M. and Turner, T. (2001) *Learning to Teach in Secondary Schools*, 3rd edn, London: Routledge. Chapter 3, Unit 3.1, deals with aspects of explanation.

Sousa, D. A. (2001) *How the Brain Learns*, 2nd edn, Thousand Oaks: Corwin.

Wragg, E. C. and Brown, G. (1993) *Explaining*, London: Routledge. A very useful self-help text.

Feedback

Students need to know how well they have done on tasks set. Feedback should be given promptly. All written work should be responded to. Helpful comments should be made to students on the way that they have tackled tasks, as well as on what they have achieved. All comments should be positive or constructive so that students can improve their response.

Feedback is the provision of an evaluation on a piece of work or action. The feedback can be formal or informal and can come from a variety of sources. The usual person to provide feedback is the teacher. There are occasions when appreciation is shown by others, such as parents as a result of reading a school report, or the head teacher about work or behaviour, or other adults working in the classroom or peers.

In your lessons you will provide informal feedback through the talks you have as you respond in whole class, group and individual situations. Encouraging students' explanation about a task and the work they have done will help them to articulate their views. If you can then encourage students to suggest what action needs to be taken you are beginning to establish an approach to students' self-evaluation. Effective feedback should be constructive. It is usual to start with something positive then move on to a more critical view. The lesson should end with each student being aware of how he/she can move forward.

Probably the most effective feedback is speaking on a one-to-one basis. You can have a dialogue with the individual student. However, in the time available, this is not always (or often) possible. Marking (written feedback) is a more traditional way of providing individual feedback. It is particularly useful when you have large classes and cannot speak to all individuals during the lesson time. It also allows you to respond to students from a distance (marking away from the classroom). Another form of feedback includes filling in competitive charts. Tangible rewards for behaviour (e.g. house points) is also a form of feedback. All these are extrinsic reward systems which assume the students appreciate the approval of others.

Links

Communication about learning
Competition
Marking
Motivation
Rewards
Thinking skills

Strategies

- Ensure feedback is given promptly.
- Offer constructive comments to the whole class, groups and/or individuals.
- Through questioning, encourage students to explain their thinking and actions.
- Encourage students to decide what action needs to be taken.
- Set up a reward system.
- Find opportunities for others (colleagues, parents and governors) to reward with praise.
- Improve feedback within your marking system (see *Marking*).

Development

Feedback, marking and reward are closely linked topics and need to be examined together, although one can be targeted whilst the others are maintained. In schools, increasingly, value is being put on the quality and type of feedback. It is important that constructive feedback offers a balance to the increasing number of summative tests in the English system. Learning takes place more successfully when there is a dialogue between students and their teacher and between students and their peers. Talking about what they understand so far about a topic often clarifies issues. The opportunity to reflect on and rectify errors is tremendously important because students make errors at the limits of their learning and they need to establish correct understanding.

Smith (2001) suggests that if students give themselves feedback about the tasks that they are doing as they go along, then learning will be more established and connected in their brains. This feedback could be a parallel account of what is happening but it could be reflective, linked to previous experience or making hypotheses, each of which is a powerful support for learning.

Further reading

Smith, A. (2001) 'What the most recent brain research tells us about learning' in Banks, F. and Shelton Mayes, A. (Eds) *Early Professional Development for Teachers*, London: David Fulton/Open University.

TTA Standard

3.2.2.

Formative assessment (monitoring students' learning)

Most assessment in the classroom is formative, because teachers are trying to build on what students know, and to sort out misconceptions. Formative assessment occurs in several 'time frames'. From minute to minute you will be making decisions in the light of the learners' responses, at the end of the lesson or day you will be assessing students' performance, your own teaching, and planning future action. Medium term assessments and planning will also be part of the analysis which will feed into future planning.

A reasonable assessment expectation in an oral, whole class situation, is to note exceptionally good and exceptionally weak responses and get a general 'feel' for whole class understanding. When working orally with the whole class there are very few situations where it is possible to assess everyone's understanding. Group work or written responses provide a greater opportunity to observe or monitor students' performance. A group objective is a closer match to the individual student's ability and therefore progress is expected and more likely to occur. In some lessons it is possible for the teacher to focus on a group and collect useful data.

It might be that the same learning objective(s) are visited in several lessons so it is easier to build a picture of the class over a short period of time. Also, the objective is often returned to in the medium term in the form of assessments such as problems and tests.

A teacher may choose to assess what students know and can do prior to running a topic so that he/she can set more meaningful objectives in medium- and short-term planning.

Assessments can be formal, such as tests and exams, or informal such as talking and observing, but will be *formative* if you take action on the results. Formative assessments are a vital part of the cycle of effective teaching. They are used to inform your next planning and teaching as well as recording individual progress.

Links

Active learning
Differentiation
Evaluating lessons
Feedback
Medium-term planning
Recording individual progress
Summative assessment
Target setting

Strategies

- Observe and question students and respond appropriately to their answers and level of understanding.
- Assess and act upon the learning that has and has not taken place in a lesson (recording and future planning).
- Select appropriate information to record informally and formally (consider purpose).
- Use formative assessment on your own teaching skills (self evaluation).

Development

Assessment is used for many different purposes and therefore it is important that you select a form of assessment which provides you with the information you need.

Further reading

For a good summary of the purposes and principles of assessment refer to:
Raffan, J. and Ruthen, K. (2000) 'Monitoring, assessment, recording, reporting and accountability', in Beck, J. and Earl, M. (Eds) *Key Issues in Secondary Education*, London: Cassell.
Capel, S. Leask, M. and Turner, T. (2001) *Learning to Teach in Secondary Schools*, 3rd edn, London: Routledge. Unit 6.1, 'Assessment and accountability' (by Terry Haydn) is a useful introduction.

TTA Standard

3.2.2.

Gender

Gender is as much about how we dress as it is about biological factors. To be seen as a man or a woman will be determined by the rules that a society has for these at a moment in time. Your experience of gender will be influenced by your upbringing. It is also likely that your experience will be different to that experienced by those who brought you up. Your schooling, your friends and your experience of work all make your experience of being a man or a woman unique. In your teaching recognize that your uniqueness is both an advantage and a disadvantage. As a teacher you will have a set of expectations about the students you teach. Your gender, like your position in society and your race, raises expectations in those who you teach. The differences in attitudes between you and them may be considerable. Some students have learned from the home to disregard women. Some have learned to disregard men. It should be noted that achievement for girls in the UK seems to be out-stripping that of boys at many stages. Your awareness about gender will inform your teaching as gender influences the way students behave and learn. Smith, (2001, p. 120) quoting work by Moir and Jessell (1993) has a useful summary of the differences. These include:

boys are better at spatial reasoning, girls are better at language;
girls talk before boys;
boys talk and play more with inanimate objects;
girls read character and social clues better;
girls talk their way through maths problems, boys work non-verbally;
girls are better at verbal activity, boys have better general maths ability;
boys need more space than girls;
boys have a shorter attention span – the list goes on.

Knowing about these means that you can choose methods, resources and examples that will help your learners.

Links

Equal opportunities
Ethnicity
Learning styles

Strategies

- Teach to take into account gender differences.
- Use methods that stimulate both verbal and non-verbal learning.
- Use both visual aids and verbal instruction.
- Break learning into small steps, give opportunities to undertake whole tasks.
- Give tasks that demand an emotional response, role play, discussion and debate, 'how would you feel if ...'.
- Aim for a balance of activities that appeals to girls and to boys.
- Get students to challenge their preferred ways of learning by doing tasks that make them feel less comfortable.

Further reading

Hill, D. and Cole, M. (Eds) (1999) *Promoting Equality in Secondary Schools,* London: Cassell.

Smith, A. (2001) 'The strategies that accelerate learning in the classroom' in Banks, F. and Shelton Mayes, A. (Eds) (2001) *Early Professional Development for Teachers,* London: Open University/David Fulton.

TTA Standard

3.3.14.

Group work

In many aspects of life we are required to work with others, so it is important that students learn how to co-operate with other students on tasks. Because many school situations require individual learning and achievement, it is easy to overlook opportunities to work as a team and to work in different teams. It is interesting to see:

who takes the lead in group work?
who has the ideas?
who comes up with the solutions?
who does the work leading to the presentation stage?

With carefully structured groups, the teacher can foster these collaborative work skills.

Reading tasks, problem solving, role-plays and presentations are good settings for group work. You will want to make sure that everyone is engaged, so both the choice of task and the size of the group must enable this to happen. When introducing a class to group work, it is often useful to start with pairs and threes. Teach them how to work collaboratively on the tasks you set. As they become more competent, increase the group size. For example, you can get pairs to form groups of four to report on what they have found out.

Groups are often created to allow for differentiation of work. In this situation groups of like ability are placed together and provided with the same work. Even though they may be sitting together, they may not be expected to work together. The work set may be individual, and not require the group to co-operate. Consider what your expectations are in such a situation, are they allowed to confer or assist each other?

Links
Differentiation
Problem solving
Skills and strategies
Social development
Whole class teaching

Strategies
- Plan opportunities for group work in appropriate settings.
- Organize groups as well as allowing for free choice on occasions.
- For collaborative group work, teach students ways of working and choose tasks that are appropriate for team work.
- Use ability groups when work needs to be differentiated.
- Vary the groups according to the tasks.

Development
Bennett and Dunne (1992) state there are three issues to be taken into account when planning co-operative group work;

the interaction between social and cognitive intentions of the grouping;
the type of task required; and
the match or appropriateness of the task to the students in the group.

The social/academic benefits of legitimizing talk ought to help with establishing the task and in motivating students to complete their contribution. Sometimes the group dynamics are not always positive and the team pulls in different directions. Sometimes this requires teacher intervention to enable the group to sort its problems out. Sometimes you will need to re-arrange the membership to get tasks completed.

Even if your school streams or sets for your subject, you may experience a wide range of ability in your classes. Deciding who goes into which group in English or maths, may not be entirely appropriate for your subject. Mixed ability groups can also be used in appropriate situations. With each class it is important for the teacher to decide the grouping that is appropriate for the work that is to be done. See Turner (2001) and Boaler and Williams (2001) for more on this issue.

Further reading

Bennett, N. and Dunne, E. (1992) *Managing Classroom Groups*, Hemel Hempstead: Simon and Schuster.

Boaler, J. and Williams, D. (2001) 'Streaming, setting and mixed ability teaching' in Dillon, J. and Maguire, M. (Eds) *Becoming a Teacher: Issues in Secondary Teaching*, 2nd edn, Buckingham: Open University Press. This chapter deals with the issues of ability grouping.

Turner, T. (2001) 'Unit 4.1 Pupil grouping, progression and differentiation' in Capel, S., Leask, M. and Turner, T. *Learning to Teach in Secondary Schools*, 3rd edn, London: Routledge, has an account of ways in which students are grouped.

TTA Standard

3.3.3.

Harassment

See *Bullying*.

Homework

There are varying practices in schools about issuing homework. At its most positive it should be seen as an opportunity to establish the practice of study in the home environment. It should be a vehicle for building independent learning. The content should be engaging and possibly relevant to the environment the students are working in. It should not rely on the provision of resources from home (*Equal opportunities*). The amount should be reasonable within a set time limit and the homework should have a clear schedule so that parents know what is expected and can therefore support your expectations. Completed work should be expected and encouragement and praise be given both at home and school. The work should also be seen or followed up in school to show that it is valued and makes a useful contribution to learning. It should be strongly linked to the learning taking place in school and the students should have a clear understanding of what they are expected to do.

Links
Completed work
Equal opportunities
Independent learning

Strategies
- Be clear about the time to be spent on the homework.
- If possible, inform parents of the homework schedule.
- Make sure the work is appropriate for the environment in which they will be working.
- Link the work to what is being learnt in class.
- Expect the work to be completed, mark it or follow it up in class.
- Praise completion and good work.
- Try not to give finishing off as homework.
- If possible, choose something which the students find engaging to do.

Development
Parents and schools have different viewpoints about homework. Some schools believe that their students need a large amount of independent study work. On the other hand some parents believe that academic work should be completed in school and home is for other leisure type activities. From the students' viewpoint, life should be a balance between freedom of choice and study.

One issue is the extent to which your students are supported in their homework. If parents, or siblings; or home tutors are involved, the work completed at home may be much better than in lessons.

Some schools discourage teachers from sending home 'finishing off' as they believe that either the teacher has not made a good judgement about the amount of work set or that allowing 'finishing off' encourages students to delay work until they get home.

Further discussion could be had on the type of work set. Do we need students to work through twenty examples or should they return prepared to discuss how they worked out one example? Is it possible to complete this particular work in that particular home environment? Some places have set up 'homework clubs' which students attend after school. This is particularly for students whose parents are out at work or who do not have an easy home study environment.

Further reading

The DfES (England and Wales) have issued useful guidance on homework. It can be found on www.dfes.gov.uk/homework/

Muijs, D. and Reynolds, D. (2001) *Effective Teaching: Evidence and Practice*, London: Paul Chapman, has a useful and practical discussion on the effective use of homework.

TTA Standard

3.3.12.

ICT (Information and Communication Technology)

ICT is playing an increasing role within teaching, as society becomes more computer literate and dependent on technology in both work and leisure activities. In school there are two strands of technology use. The first is using ICT to support the organization of and quality outputs in managing your teaching. The second is using ICT with students to support a range of subject learning and to develop their ICT skills.

Your teaching can be supported by using ICT to:

• plan medium-term (and short-term) documents;
• create and record assessments;
• prepare teaching materials;
• prepare display materials;
• access current initiatives and information (internet).

Working with students, ICT can be used to:

• enhance subject learning through use of hardware, software and the internet;
• develop students' ICT skills through hands-on experience.

When working with students you may be using only one computer in the classroom or a suite of computers in a special room. You need to consider carefully the organization of each of these situations to get the most from them.

ICT encompasses a range of hardware including electronic white board, video, DVD, CD-ROM, computer, overhead projector, tape recorder and programme controlled toys and gadgets, all of which can be utilized effectively within the classroom in appropriately planned contexts.

Links

Lesson plan structure
Medium-term planning
Resources
Working with other adults

Strategies

- Plan ICT use into your lessons at the medium-term planning stage.
- When working in a suite, structure your lesson, have a clear objective and a teaching input.
- When using one computer in the classroom select relevant programs and carefully organize how students will get a turn. Use other students to support skill learning and an understanding of program instructions.
- Use one computer as a whole class teaching aid.
- Try to provide a range of ICT experiences.
- Use ICT lessons to promote skills.
- Use ICT within lessons to promote subject learning.
- Check it all works before the students arrive.
- Have explored for yourself the programs you are going to use with the students.

Development

With the increase of computer accessibility, particularly to the World Wide Web and its vast stores of information, we will be forced to reassess our teaching approach to knowledge and the balance between knowledge and skills. Another further issue is raised when we ask who has access to computers at home? Will the lack of computer access disadvantage some students? Will schools provide after-school access in the same way that they are beginning to provide homework clubs?

A further interesting aspect of computer use by students is the programs which they use. What do they learn from them? Does computer use encourage independent study? Do certain programmes promote thinking skills? It is important to consider the purpose of a programme when you plan to use it in class, in exactly the same way you decide about other activities you ask students to do. There are many types of programmes including, games, information giving, practice and problem solving.

In England trainee teachers must know how to teach ICT and 'know how to use ICT effectively, both to teach their subject and to support their wider professional role' (DfES, 2002, pp. 7–8). Alongside these expectations for initial teacher training, there are other government funded programmes for practising teachers, for example, the New Opportunities Fund (NOF) and the British Educational Communications Technology Agency (BECTa). In some schools students are using laptops in the classroom with interesting results. Looking into the future, it is possible to envisage every student having access to their own laptop both in school and at home.

Further reading

Ager, R. (2000) *The Art of Information and Communications Technology for Teachers*, London: David Fulton.

BBC Education www.bbc.co.uk/schools (useful for internet resources for teachers).

BECTa can be found at www.becta.org.uk

Department for Education and Skills (DfES) (2002) *Qualifying to Teach: Professional Standards for Qualified Teacher Status and Requirements for Initial Teacher Training* TPU 0803/02-02 London:TTA (weblink www.canteach.gov.uk).

National Grid for Learning (NGfL) www.ngfl.gov.uk a gateway to educational resources on the internet.

NOF information can be found at www.canteach.gov.uk

QCA site www.qca.org.uk a useful site for schemes of work.

Teachernet www.teachernet.gov.uk a teacher resource and staff professional development site, including research.

Watson, D. (2001) 'Information and Communication Technology: Policy and Practice' in Dillon, J. and Maguire, M. (Eds) *Becoming a Teacher: Issues in Secondary Teaching*, 2nd edn, Buckingham: Open University Press.

www.curriculumonline.gov.uk gives easy access to digital learning materials.

TTA Standard
3.3.10.

Inclusion

The first thoughts about inclusion often concern students with Special Educational Needs, but inclusive policy is wider than this. It is about all students who are at risk of exclusion through:

> non-attendance – truancy, long-term illness, long holidays in term time, teenage pregnancy;
> disaffection – students who attend but take no interest in learning, students who bully and their victims;
> formal exclusion – students whose conduct has been unacceptable in school through persistent defiance of legitimate school rules;
> disadvantage – poverty, poor housing, nutrition, poor parenting, students 'looked after' by the state;
> student mobility – travellers' children, asylum seekers, immigrants.

A social justice view of education takes the position that high quality education for all is an inclusive goal. Social justice has at its roots the idea that economic, racial and gender discrimination are not acceptable. It follows that action needs to be taken to ensure that everyone is able to be included. This implies that strong partnerships and working relationships are needed between parents, students, teachers and the different agencies beyond schools. In the UK, the aim is that mainstream schools should meet the needs of as many students as possible.

A useful concept when thinking about inclusion is that of *barriers to learning*. Prejudice and stereotyping are often significant in creating and maintaining these barriers. Perhaps you'll hear some of this in school. Students who are difficult to teach can evoke negative responses. Rather than thinking about what students can achieve we sometimes think of what they cannot do. The ways in which students are referred to often gives clues about the mindset of the speaker. For example, 'This is John, he has difficulty in seeing the print in most books, so he uses large print books', has a more positive and therefore more inclusive feel, than saying, 'a partially sighted pupil' or 'a blind pupil'. What inclusion is about is looking for ways of reducing the barriers to learning that exist for students who present more of a challenge to school staff.

Links

Connexions
Differentiation
Equal opportunities
Expectations about students' learning
Special Educational Needs
Teaching in teams
Working with other adults

Strategies

Consider the ways you can reduce barriers to learning by:

- Looking for positive attributes in students who are difficult to teach.
- Praising any improvement – rewarding effort and celebrating achievement – even when for many students these would be considered unimportant, e.g. sitting still for two minutes is a real achievement for some youngsters!
- Being careful about the assumptions you make, e.g. hearing a noise behind you and blaming the 'normal culprit' when he or she is innocent can make it worthwhile for that student to misbehave in future. 'Mr X ain't fair, he's always picking on me' (sic) gives some students the excuse they need not to conform to the rules.
- Use classroom assistants effectively.
- Building your knowledge about the difficulties that cause some students to find learning in school problematic.

Development

Can social inclusion happen? Three ideas – social inclusion, educational inclusion and inclusive schools – are central to UK government policy. These rules are nearly all about improving education provision. Publicly funded schools in England have been set targets for examination success. Alongside this, a rigorous inspection system has required teachers to become better at their work, i.e. to teach *every* student more effectively. This has been accompanied by many other measures to begin to enable much greater inter-agency co-operation. Educational inclusion, with the underlying ideas from social inclusion, is about meeting the different needs of as many students as possible in mainstream schooling. This happens in many ways. For example:

Many more classroom assistants are employed to work alongside teachers to support students either individually because of special need or to support groups of students with learning difficulties, in particular EAL, but also where standards in English, mathematics or science are thought to be unacceptably low.
Schools have been asked to consider carefully all the ways they can keep students in school. Many schools have sought ways to encourage students to arrive on time and to be ready to learn, through things like breakfast clubs. Rewards for a full week's attendance help to reduce unauthorized absence from school. Students with unacceptable behaviour, who are in danger of exclusion, may get extra support to keep them where they can continue school learning.

The idea of an inclusive school that will meet the needs of many students in a variety of ways; within special classes; through support for individuals; differentiation in the curriculum; and carefully thought through teaching, is an idea that is exciting.

Further reading

Clough, P. and Corbett, J. (2000) *Theories of Inclusive Education A Students' Guide*, London: Paul Chapman.
Department for Education and Employment (DfEE) (1997) *Excellence for all Children, Meeting Special Educational Needs*, London: DfEE.
Department for Education and Skills (DfES) (2001) *Schools Achieving Success*, London: HMSO.
Lorenz, S. (2002) *First Steps in Inclusion*, London: David Fulton. This handbook has some excellent starting places for making the ideas of social justice work.
See DfES webpages for the most up-to-date information about SEN and the Connexions service http//:inclusion.ngfl.gov.uk

TTA Standard

3.1.2.

Independent learning

One of the hardest but most creditable achievements of a teacher is to help his or her students along the road to independent learning. Lots of things have to come together to achieve this goal. Students need to want to do good work and behave well because they feel it is right to conduct themselves in this way.

They have to learn to be decision makers. They have to become involved in the work they do because they want to do it, not because the teacher says all the time that, 'you have to do it'. They have to know what they want to achieve and therefore why they are doing the work. They should want to conduct themselves well in classes and to treat each other with respect, because it feels right to them.

As a teacher you need to give them opportunities to exercise these choices, but it will not happen if you just remove all the structures and discipline. Self-discipline comes through recognizing what discipline is. The teacher creates order and gradually encourages more independent decision making through discussion and guidance. There may be 'whole class' stages of this progression or, existing side-by-side, individuals who are ready to take on more responsibility.

This has implications as to how you organize the learning in your classes. You must decide who is ready for 'the greater freedom'. As students become young adults they become more able to make these decisions, often with your advice and the help of other adults. Your knowledge about your students' ability to handle autonomy will be based in part on the understanding you have about their emotional and intellectual development.

Links

Active learning
Discipline
Emotional development
Expectations about students' learning
Intellectual development
Key skills
Motivation
Problem solving
Self-assessment by students

Strategies

• Find ways of allowing responsible students to be more involved in decisions about their work.

- Discuss expected behaviour and work outputs in whole class settings.
- Be clear about why students are doing particular pieces of work (purpose as well as objective).
- Ensure certain resources are accessible without permission and if appropriate there are choices about what to use.
- Try to make sure all decision making does not have to pass through you.
- In suitable situations allow students to help each other.

Development

Encouraging students to be independent learners is a long-term goal. It is not easy to achieve and you as a teacher will need to think carefully about the 'campaign'. Some students enjoy working at projects and are happy to do so on their own. They always seem to be motivated and engage in anything you offer. Initially, many in your classes will sit there waiting for you to tell them what to do next. They are very teacher dependent. Some teachers like their students to be like this as it offers strong control and they are happy for this to be the status quo for all the year. Whilst control is vital, over and above that, self-control by students is even better. An important question to ask about each class you teach is, 'Could I leave the room and be confident that the students will continue to work?'. To achieve this the students need to be able to operate independently of the teacher. This is achieved by promoting a range of skills and understanding. Students need to be confident about their own decision making, they need to be skilled at selecting and using information, they need to know the purpose of the task, they need to want to engage in the task, and they need to have work to move on to if they complete the task early. These are just a few of the opportunities that have to be regularly promoted and praised throughout the year if you want students to manage their own work.

Further reading

Bobbitt Nolen, S. (1995) 'Teaching for Autonomous Learning' in Desforges, C. (Ed.) *An Introduction to Teaching*, Oxford: Blackwell. Although written about primary aged children this chapter explores this issue using a number of different perspectives.

TTA Standard

3.3.3.

Instruction

Letting students know that you're ready to start has to be one of the first things you'll learn to do. You'll need a procedure for gaining everyone's undivided attention. In large or noisy spaces two hand claps is a good way of gaining attention without shouting. Your instructions need to be brief, clear and positive. Your tone needs to be confident and pleasant. Often you'll need to reinforce your instruction by rephrasing and directing your comments to particular students. For example,

> (*Teacher claps twice.*) 'Can I have everyone's attention, thanks. Abdul, Shahida, Martin and Susan, look this way, thanks. Now, when I tell you, I want one person from each group to collect the apparatus from me. Everyone else in the group needs to clear anything that's on your table that's not needed for the task. Is that clear? (*Slight pause as the teacher looks round to ensure that students are attending.*) One set of apparatus and one prepared table. Start now'.

Give generalized instructions once, for example, 'Everyone start work now'. Follow this up by telling a particular student what you want, 'John, I've told you to get started, get on with your work'. Don't nag by giving the same instruction to everyone over and over again. Acknowledge those who have heeded your instructions with a smile, a gesture and some quiet praise. If you fall into the trap of giving the same instruction over and over again, your students soon realize that you are prepared to do this and don't bother to listen the first time.

You'll also be preparing worksheets and other written material which instructs students to do something. You'll need to know how best to do this for the whole range of ability. Keeping the language simple, sentences short and being really clear is the key. You may have to prepare two or three versions before you get this right, trialling them with students whom you know find reading instructions hard. Even then you'll need to have the instruction read to some students. Another student may do this or you might use a taped version or use a classroom assistant.

Links

Demonstration by the teacher
Discipline

Explaining
Independent learning
Timing within lessons
Transitions
Whole class teaching
Working with other adults

Strategies

When instructing students:

- Have a clear signal that gets everyone's attention.
- Be pleasant and confident, stand still, get eye contact, smile, use a clear tone of voice.
- Be precise, be clear yourself what you want done and how it is to be done.
- Be brief.
- Be positive, for example use 'thanks' rather than 'please'. ('Thanks' often demonstrates that you are confident that your instruction will be followed, 'please' can have a pleading quality.)
- Reinforce the instruction through repeating it.
- Deal separately with anyone who has not yet complied.
- Quiet praise to individuals who do as they are asked promptly helps to build a positive working atmosphere.
- Written instructions for your teaching need to be kept simple:
  by using direct language, avoid negatives, explain technical terms;
  use short sentences, repeat the subject, avoiding 'it' and 'they', (e.g. most students will find 'The cats woke up. The cats went out'. easier to read than 'The cats woke up. They went out');
  use a clear type face (Arial is a good example and 12 point or larger is helpful);
  use a straightforward layout.
- Check that your written instructions have been understood by the students.
- Be prepared to trial written instructions to get them to a level that most students can read.
- Students who find reading hard should have appropriate help.

Development

Some instructions are to do with class management. They make the day-to-day organization of the minutiae of teaching and learning possible. Instructions are also part of lesson planning. Both are part of making learning easier. However, you'll also want to consider how you encourage students to make decisions about how, when and where to do things as independent learning.

Further reading

Capel, S., Leask, M. and Turner, T. (2001) *Learning to Teach in Secondary Schools*, 3rd edn, London: Routledge. Chapter 3, Section 3.1, is about communicating with students.
Thody, A., Gray, B. and Bowden, D. (2000) *The Teacher's Survival Guide*, London: Continuum. Part 2 has some sound advice and some further pointers.

Intellectual development

How we learn is a focus of development studies. Development theorists have different but often complementary ideas about intellectual growth. Behaviourists, however, offer another idea. There are four theories which you should know about.

The *behaviourist theories* (from the 1920s onwards, with psychologists Pavlov, Skinner and Bandura as the more important names) emphasized change in behaviour as the outcome of learning. The stimulus – response model is clearly seen in much direct instruction, including the management of behaviour.

Jean Piaget's theory of *cognitive development* has two essential elements. He suggests that our minds actively seek to make sense of the world. Our cognitive structures (our minds) are *adaptations* which take knowledge and make it fit with the world about us. He studied many pre-school children. His observations about the mistakes that they make, their misunderstandings which arose from their point of view about how things work, lead him to suggest that 'cognitive development is a process of revision: children revise their knowledge to provide an increasingly better fit to reality'. (Keenan, 2002, p. 37). His second big idea was to suggest that we move through four different stages. The knowledge structures used by learners are relatively similar and stable throughout each stage. At the *sensorimotor* stage, birth to about 2 years, 'the infant thinks about the world through their actions on it' (Keenan, 2002 p. 37). The random actions of the child become increasingly more organized and systematic. The child becomes more able to handle abstract ideas and moves into the *preoperational stage*, 2–7 years. At this stage the child becomes able to handle thinking through symbolic representation. In the *concrete operational stage*, 7–12 years, logical thought becomes well established. The *formal operational stage*, adolescence, sees the development of abstract thought. In secondary schools you will find students at all the stages that Piaget identified, although most will be in the concrete operational or formal operational stage. It is worth ignoring the age labels and thinking about how students learn in your subject. Sometimes students struggle with new concepts and will work at a lower stage until they grasp it. Sometimes students work at a higher stage than you might have predicted. These days this influential theory is increasingly criticized. You'll discover that the child as a solitary learner has little or no support these days.

Lev Vygotsky's *sociocultural* theory of development also sees children as active explorers of the world in which they find themselves. He suggested that it is the social interactions with the people that children meet that make it possible for learning to happen. He also believed that there is a pattern to development, that children move from working with others, to working things out for themselves, characterized by self-talk where the child will talk him/herself through a task. He also observed that parents and teachers, when working with children, tailored what they said, the way they said it and what they did to support the child's development.

Information processing models and theories seem, after an uncertain start, to be really useful. These arise from computer modelling. *Connectionist* models that match brain-function to learning tasks seems promising. For example, the use of advanced organizers to help make connections between what the child already knows and what has to be learned is one aspect of this theory.

All these theories and models have something to offer teachers. It would be impossible to think about teaching and learning without them. Many teachers confirm, that at about 14 years, the way in which students learn does become different. They are more independent and can often be keen to encounter new learning and new ways of thinking. We need to think of all our students as active learners. We know that the interventions we make can help or hinder learning and we are beginning to understand how knowledge of the physiology of the brain can help. Clearly, as this is the briefest of brief outlines, you'll want to learn more.

Further reading

Head, J. (2001) 'Adolescence' in Dillon, J. and Maguire, M. (Eds) *Becoming a Teacher: Issues in Secondary Teaching*, Buckingham: Open University Press, pp. 136–41 is a useful introduction.

Turner, T. (2001) Unit 4 'Cognitive development' in Capel, S., Leask, M. and Turner, T. *Learning to Teach in Secondary Schools*, 3rd edn, London: Routledge, pp. 159–60 – p. 177 is also useful.

For more detail consult:

Keenan, T. (2002) *An Introduction to Child Development*, London: Sage.

Meece, J. L. (1997) *Child and Adolescent Development for Educators*, New York: McGraw Hill.

Muijs, D. and Reynolds, D. (2001) *Effective Teaching: Evidence and Practice*, London: Paul Chapman.

Sousa, D. A. (2001) *How the Brain Learns*, Thousand Oaks: Corwin is recommended for a straightforward introduction to the brain.

Smith, A. (2001) 'The strategies that accelerate learning in the classroom' in Banks, F. and Shelton Mayes, A. (Eds) *Early Professional Development for Teachers*, London: Open University/David Fulton, offers other ways that theory links to practice.

Vygotsky, L. (1991) *Thought and Language* (translation edited by Kuzulin, A.) Cambridge, MA: MIT Press.

TTA Standard

2.4.

Intervention

Intervention is when the teacher engages with groups or individuals in an attempt to move them on with the work they are doing. The most successful interventions enable students to extend their thinking. These usually come in the form of questioning, prompts and requests for explanations from the students. Try not to give immediate solutions which is deflating and demotivating. The students will not develop their own problem solving skills if everything is too easy or straightforward. We need students to develop their process skills and take ownership of the work they do.

Intervention can also be considered in the context of behaviour. By an early intervention much poor behaviour can be prevented; a deteriorating situation can be avoided. As you get to know a class there will be clues as to the way things are going. For example, a change in the type of noise, 'known offenders' getting restless, or students disengaged from the task because it is too hard. If you sense anything like this, act upon it quickly. Make them aware you are keeping an eye on them. Be sure that you are accurate in your identification. Students who you falsely accuse of misbehaviour will resent it. If possible do not let the situation deteriorate to the point where you get into disciplinary routines.

Links

Group work
Independent learning
Listening and responding to students
Questioning

Strategies

- Decide or explore with a student how much help they really need.
- Try to promote students thinking for themselves by choosing a prompt or question type of intervention.
- Try to anticipate problems by early intervention.
- Spot check on students most likely to misbehave.

Development

Vygotsky (1934), a Russian writer and educationalist who lived in the first half of the twentieth century developed a theory known as the 'zone of proximal development' (ZPD). This term describes the influence the teacher has when working with a student. The greater the improvement when working with the teacher as opposed to the student working on his own, the greater the zone of proximal development, which, Vygotsky thought, was an indicator of potential. An example of this would be an able student dramatically extending and expressing their understanding due to the teacher's intervention with questioning and prompts.

'Scaffolding' is the current term used to describe teacher intervention to support learning. It is the provision of structures by the teacher to enable learning to take place. This might be a light touch such as introducing a task, giving verbal prompts as the task unfolds or more strongly structured intervention such as a demonstration of the procedure to be followed. Over time a teacher might remove the 'scaffolding' as he/she feels that the concept is established. One can see how scaffolding has close links to Vygotsky's zone of proximal development. Mercer and Dawes (2001) researched how teacher and student–student language supports learning. They draw upon the theories of Vygotsky and scaffolding to illuminate the dialogues which take place in the classroom.

Further reading

Mercer, N. and Dawes, L. (2001) 'Dialogues for teaching and learning' in Banks, F. and Shelton Mayes, A. (eds) *Early Professional Development for Teachers*, London: David Fulton/Open University.

Vygotsky, L. (1991) *Thought and Language* (translation edited by Kuzulin, A.) Cambridge, MA: MIT Press.

Wood, D. and Middleton, D. (1975) 'A study of assisted problem-solving' in *British Journal of Psychology*, 66: 2, (181–91).

Key skills

In England, all secondary schools are expected to include Key Skills' teaching across all subjects. Certification in six areas, *application of number, information technology, working with others, improving own learning* and *performance* and *problem solving* is available from Key Stage 4. Key Skills give you the opportunity to teach students how to learn within the work you'll do in your subject. Teaching these learning skills in the context of your work should be a benefit.

Links

Active learning
Independent learning
Learning styles
National qualifications

Strategies

- Plan within your subject team and across other subjects and year groups to ensure that all six areas are covered systematically.
- Teach students how to use a key skill in the context of your subject work (e.g. integrate key skills within the subject tasks you set).
- Keep the key skills you are teaching closely related to what you have to teach in the subject.
- Link skills wherever you can (for example, communication, working with others, problem solving and reflection on learning can be taught through one area of the content you are teaching).

- Develop resources, readings, worksheets, WWW guides that limit and guide searches, which relate to the content of your subject and can be used on more than one occasion.
- Teach students the skills they need to use the resources you've prepared.
- Develop resources that can be used without teacher intervention e.g. for homework.
- Set students work that enables them to work in pairs on specified tasks.
- Teach students to evaluate their own learning in a systematic way, e.g. working towards giving them the ability to check their work against the marking criteria, in small steps.
- Include self-assessment sheets in some work that you set.
- Give feedback on how students learned (the learning strategies used) as well as what they learned (the content).
- Set targets on learning as well as the content you want them to learn.

Development

One of the consequences of teaching students how to learn in your subject is that they will become better able to learn, more critical and clearer about the need for evidence to back opinions. They may well become more independent learners. This is generally thought to be useful but it may also mean that you are challenged in what you say about your subject by your, now, more confident students. This is something to be celebrated but you'll need to prepare for this greater autonomy in your students.

Further reading

http://atschool.eduweb.co.uk/ufa/othersub.htm is an example of one of many websites that suggest ideas for including Key Skills. This site is about maths.

www.curriculumonline.gov.uk for access to digital information.

www.standards.dfes.gov.uk/keystage3 is the key site for DfES guidance.

TTA Standards

2.1d, 2.3, 3.2.2, 3.3.2c,d, 3.3.3.

Learning environment

See *Purposeful working atmosphere*.

Learning objectives

When planning in the medium-term and the short-term it is important to identify what you want students to know and be able to do. A learning objective can be about gaining a new piece of knowledge or acquiring a new skill. The objective of the lesson might be to consolidate or assess a piece of learning. Learning objectives for a lesson might start with the words:

to introduce ... to be able to ... to practise ... to apply ... to revise ... to assess understanding of ...

They are all focused on what the expected outcome of the students' learning is. They involve a process of learning rather than stating the completion of a particular task. The tasks used are the vehicles for the learning. For example, 'to introduce the use of prefixes' is a learning objective as opposed to 'complete exercise 10' which does not state what learning will take place. Some lessons have sub-objectives within the group task phase of the lesson. This allows for differentiation to take place.

Once you have a clear and manageable objective, the planning and teaching become easier and more focused. The assessment becomes easier too, as you know what you are looking for in the student's performance. It is probable that the assessment criterion for the lesson is similar to the learning objective, or is a part of it. It could be appropriate to record whether particular students have met your objective. Certainly it is appropriate for you, as teacher, to evaluate whether the class and groups have met objectives so that you can feed this into your planning (see *Evaluating lessons*). In practice this will mean that you draw from both your scheme and records to plan a follow on lesson.

Links

Active learning
Curriculum
Differentiation
Evaluating lessons
Formative assessment
Lesson plan structure
Medium-term planning

Strategies

- Choose an objective that describes the required learning rather than the task.
- To differentiate work, if necessary, use sub-objectives.
- Make the objective reasonably achievable within one or two lessons.
- Plan objectives that build on previous learning.
- Have a cycle of introduction, consolidation and application rather than a new objective each lesson.
- Link learning objectives to assessment criteria.

Development

Students are more likely to learn if your objective is clear and manageable and the purpose is clear to them. Both of these need to be made explicit at the start of the lesson. Some would advocate writing the objective on the board. It depends on whether you think this is an effective strategy for the students you teach. Some teachers share their objectives with the parents of their students, e.g. identifying the learning outcomes for homework or the work to be covered in the next half term.

A series of carefully constructed objectives should lead to progression in learning and will provide strong evidence for inspection in medium- and short-term planning. You will have to make decisions about worthwhile diversions from your original planning. Maybe the students failed to grasp your objective and you want to revisit it the next lesson. Maybe a really interesting aspect developed and you feel that the students will learn much by pursuing it. Maybe an event occurred or a student brought a fascinating object into school. These spontaneous situations are no less valid than your planned programme. Evaluate what the students will gain from a change of programme. It is usually a positive learning experience. Just not the one you planned.

TTA Standards

3.1.1, 3.1.2, 3.2.1, 3.3.3.

Learning styles

You'll know that your preferred way of learning is unique. No-one else learns in quite the same way as you do. The same as each student you teach will have a preferred way of learning. Our challenge is to match our teaching to the variety of learning styles* that our students may have. And, as far as we can, to give them access to all the learning styles and strategies that they may need to use.

Our five senses give us information about the world, but they don't all contribute equally to the way we learn. We may have a preference to learn visually (perhaps you doodle) – *visual learners*. Or through listening – *auditory learners*. Or prefer to manipulate materials or move about – *kinaesthetic learners*. Whichever, sensory preferences are important in an individual's learning. Your own learning style preference is likely to be the way you teach. Because of this it is really important to take account of the learning style of students by both using their preferences and extending their range. This increases their ability to learn.

Using *VAK* (visual, auditory, kinaesthetic) *learning strategies* in our teaching offers students greater opportunities of access to a range of learning styles. VAK teaching uses the following to develop:

- *Visual learning* text plus illustration, graphs, maps, visualization to improve memory, access to CD-ROMs, posters, keywords, videos, demonstrations, memory mapping (e.g. flow charts, story boards).
- *Auditory learning* opportunities to talk about the work, lectures i.e. something to listen to (radio or from an audio tape) to get the picture, spelling that recalls the pattern through sounds.
- *Kinaesthetic learning* (learning through movement) the opportunity to be active, role plays, field trips, hand movements and gestures when talking, demonstrations, designs and making tasks.

Links

Active learning
Differentiation
Displays
Intellectual development
Problem solving

---

*Authors use slightly different terms for what is essentially the same idea, for example, learning strategies, cognitive style or strategy, or style constructs. It may be helpful to think about style as what we are born with and strategy as learned.

Resources
Thinking skills

Strategies

- Recognizing different learning styles means acknowledging that learners will behave differently in lessons, e.g. kinaesthetic learners may seem to fidget more and need to be active in order to learn. This knowledge can help to explain apparent misbehaviour, the restlessness you observe, is not necessarily misbehaviour.
- Take account of your own learning style preference by deliberately using other styles in your teaching.
- Observe how students react to the different learning styles that you use so that you can extend their ability to learn from each.
- Help students to recognize their own preferred learning style and the need to develop different learning strategies through exploring and talking about these with them.

Development

This idea of cognitive styles linked to preferred ways of learning feels right, but the research base is not strong. Riding and Rayner (1998: 9) after an extensive review of the literature suggest two learning styles wholistic – analytic dimension; and verbal – imagery dimension – as valid. *Wholistic – analytic* individuals tend to organize information in wholes or parts. In a *verbal – imagery* style individuals tend to represent information through thinking verbally or in mental pictures. See Riding (2002) for ways of incorporating these styles into teaching. Gardner (1983) in his analysis recognizes seven kinds of intelligence, known as *multiple intelligences*, it is an attractive theory which suggests that human beings are problem solvers bringing different ways of thinking to different tasks. It is useful to recognize the strengths that you and those you teach have and then to think of ways of helping all of the learners to develop a wide repertoire.

Further reading

Gardner, H. (2001) 'The theory of multiple intelligences' in Banks, F. and Shelton Mayes, A. (Eds) *Early Professional Development for Teachers*, London: Open University/David Fulton. pp. 133–41. This chapter draws on Gardner's work from 1983 and work with J. Walters in 1985. It appeals to those who like 'common sense' theory!

Riding, R. (2002) *School Learning and Cognitive Style*, London: David Fulton. An authoritative and practical book that covers this area well.

Riding, R. and Rayner, S. (1998) *Cognitive Styles and Learning Strategies – Understanding Style Differences in Learning and Behaviour*, London: David Fulton. The authors provide an excellent introduction to many aspects of learning style, well backed by research.

Smith, A. (2001) 'The strategies that accelerate learning in the classroom' in Banks, F. and Shelton Mayes, A. (Eds) *Early Professional Development for Teachers*, London: Open University/David Fulton, pp. 159–77. This is an excellent summary about many aspects of learning, including learning styles.

Lesson plan structure

The lesson plan is the document on which the detailed organization of your lesson is placed. You will transfer some of your headings from the medium-term planning and you will be making decisions about timing, exact content and resources. Whatever format you use, your lesson plan headings support your thinking on:

- what you want the students to achieve during the lesson (learning objective);
- what you are going to observe and assess (assessment criteria);
- how long you are going to spend on each part of the lesson (timing);
- how and when you are going to group the students (grouping);
- what organization and resources you are going to need (resources);
- the specific nature of the content with some prompt to the teaching points you are going to make (teaching points).

It is also a good strategy to have an extension activity (extra work that does not involve new knowledge, but challenges learners) for the speedy workers in your classes. The plenary or conclusion is where you draw your lesson together and re-establish the objectives so that students know what they have learned and what still needs to be learned.

It is useful to have the lesson plan within reach during the lesson as a prompt. Putting the lesson plan in a transparent plastic folder is useful and will help in keeping it clean and easy to read. Highlighting the main points can also be useful as you may only be able to glance quickly at your plan during the lesson.

Links

Communicating clearly
Communication about learning
Curriculum
Evaluating lessons
Explaining
Group work
Instruction
Learning objectives
Long-term planning
Medium-term planning
Pace
Transitions
Whole class teaching

Strategies

- Always prepare lesson plans so that you are clear and purposeful in your teaching.
- Keep to your proposed timing unless you have an educationally valid reason for adjusting it.
- Make the objective clear to the students at the start of the lesson and return to the expected learning at the end.
- Keep your notes brief and easy to read, possibly using bullet points and highlighter.
- Maintain an assessment focus throughout the lesson.

Development

Muijs and Reynolds (2001) describe two types of lesson: direct instruction and interactive. A piece of learning might go through stages over a series of lessons and this is reflected in the balance of teacher input to students involved in task activities. This will be reflected in the timing and content of the lesson. Many people follow a three-part model which starts with whole class teaching, moves on to group work, and then returns at the end to whole class teaching. The first part of this often involves a review of previously taught connected work.

The structure of most lessons will require you to consider and plan for the following:

- learning objective;
- assessment criteria and mode;

- content;
- organization (grouping, timing and resources);
- extension activities;
- conclusion/plenary;
- evaluation.

In addition to planning what the students will be doing, it is important to decide where you will be in the lesson and what you will be doing. This is particularly relevant during the group work where it is possible to spend the whole time 'policing' the classroom when you could be offering teaching input for part of the time. However detailed your planning there will always be differences in the speed at which students work, therefore it is important to plan how you will deal productively with the early finishers and those who do not complete their work.

Further reading

Muijs, D. and Reynolds, D. (2001) *Effective Teaching: Evidence and Practice*, London: Paul Chapman.

TTA Standards

3.1.2, 3.3.3, 3.3.7.

Level descriptions

Level descriptions can be found in the assessment section of the English National Curriculum (DfEE, 2000). They are descriptions of students' attainment within each of the targets of the National Curriculum.

> *Each level describes the type and range of performance that students working at that level should characteristically demonstrate. The level descriptions provide the basis for making judgements about students' performance at the end of Key Stages 1, 2 and 3. At Key Stage 4, national qualifications are the main means of assessing attainment in national curriculum subjects.'*   (DfEE, 2000)

In assessing the level of a student's performance a 'best fit' is made of their achievements against the descriptions provided. These descriptions are drawn from the Programmes of Study (syllabus). It is anticipated that the average seven year old in England and Wales should achieve a Level 2, the average 11-year-old a Level 4 and the average 14-year-old will be at Level 5/6. At Key Stage 4 national qualifications are the means of assessing attainment in National Curriculum subjects.

Level descriptions can be used by schools as part of their internal assessment strategies and reporting requirements, but nationally, nearly all school students are assessed against these descriptions at the end of Key Stages in English, mathematics and science. Teacher assessments at these stages must be reported to parents alongside the results of the key stage tests.

Links

Curriculum
National qualifications
Summative assessment

Strategies

- Match a student's work to the National Curriculum levels.
- Ensure individual records provide sufficient information to allow a National Curriculum level to be provided in each attainment target.
- Find out what teacher assessment is required during the year and set up assessment and recording systems to evidence this.

Development

Assessing students in this summative fashion on a national scale gives parents, pupils and teachers an indication of each student's performance in relation to all the other students of his or her age in the whole country. From the school's point of view, the performance of students in the school provides feedback on how well the school is performing.

It is important for teachers to realize that tests sample a student's knowledge. 'Best fit' assessment indicates that the student is secure in a majority of the criteria but not necessarily all. Teachers' records kept against achievement (criterion referenced procedures) will probably provide the most accurate picture of what a student does and does not know. Even then it is impossible for a teacher to establish exactly what a student knows at any one time.

Further reading

www.highscope.org An example of a pre school education programme with world wide impact.

www.nc.uk.net has the most up-to-date information about level descriptions.

www.qca.org.uk/ca/texts is useful for general information on tests for England.

TTA Standards

3.1.2, 3.3.3, 3.3.7.

Linguistic development

In secondary school you will find that there are considerable differences in language skill levels between students of the same age. You may well find that while most school students operate with increasing sophistication, some are still at much earlier stages of linguistic development. For students, perhaps the majority, mastery, as against everyday usage, over speaking, listening, reading and writing has to be taught. The introduction of *Key Skills* (see entry) into English Secondary schools is a recognition of the importance of linguistic development. For example, understanding and responding to audience in speaking and writing is something that needs to be taught. Similarly, making appropriate choices of text, finding the source that answers the question precisely, learning to ask the questions for themselves is something that is learnt, most securely, through carefully structured teaching. Text messaging is a powerful example that even adults find that there are always new challenges in the area of linguistic development.

The response of babies to the pitch, rhythm and cadence of their mothers' voice, not the words, is observed from birth. By between 10–12 months the brain has become familiar with and is able to discriminate the separate sounds (phonemes) of the first language that the child hears at home. At about the same time they begin to attach meaning to words. Speech, producing at first single words, may also start at this time. Unfortunately, as English grammar has many non-standard forms, learning this takes a little longer. By 3 many children are about 90 per cent correct but many may still be learning, through the parents' correction, that, 'I hitted (sic) it.' needs to be 'I hit it'. The implication is that a language rich pre school life will advantage children.

Beyond 5 to adolescence the number of words in a child's vocabulary increases to 30,000, grammatical construction becomes more complex and, generally, the understanding and use of the full range of language use – things like *pronoun reference, metaphor, sarcasm* – become established. This knowledge is used in learning to read and write. Learning to read and write, unlike learning to speak is not a 'natural' process. Most children have to be taught to read and write. We have to learn that, for example:

the marks (letters, the spaces between words, punctuation) on the page have meaning;
the text is close to speech but not entirely the same.

One important difference is the relative permanence of print. It can be read and re-read. Learning to read and write in English, with its complex alphabetic structure means learning about exceptions as well as rules. There are 44 phonemes, but only 26 letters. Listen to the sound of 'o' in these words: one, women, who, Tom, the same letter can represent more than one sound. Then some sounds (phonemes) can be spelt in different ways, try these, by, tie, bye, high – all ways of representing 'i'. Another potential learning trap is in a word like 'cat' which sounds like one phoneme even though it is made up of three phonemes *c/a/t*. Poor readers have difficulty with these principles. However, with instruction most children have begun to read well by the age of 8. Writing sometimes lags behind this and by secondary school the gap between the most able and the least able readers and writers can be considerable. Some secondary school students will still find basic reading and writing a challenge.

Links

Adolescence
Differentiation
English as an additional language
Intellectual development
Social development

Further reading

Meece, J. L. (1997) *Child and Adolescent Development for Educators*, New York: McGraw Hill. Chapter 5, 'Language development and literacy' is very comprehensive.

Muijs, D. and Reynolds, D. (2001) *Effective Teaching: Evidence and Practice*, London: Paul Chapman, 'Literacy', Chapter 15, is an excellent summary on approaches to reading.

TTA Standard
2.4.

Listening and responding to students

The classroom is a place where two worlds meet, the world of education and the world of home. As teachers we need to create opportunities for students to link both environments and to contribute from their experience.

By listening and conversing with students they will feel valued and are more likely to contribute. If you have developed good dialogue with individuals you will have also created a good setting for learning to take place.

There is a difference between making friends with students and establishing a good working relationship. In the second you will always maintain the role of teacher, but as a teacher who is approachable and interested in the student as a person. Having students as friends is not an option until they have left school. It would be unprofessional and a breach of your duty of care (see *Relationships with pupils* for further explanation).

Links

Communicating clearly
Communication about learning
Culture
Ethnicity
Misconceptions and remedies
Questioning
Relationships with students

Strategies

• Create opportunities for students to contribute from their own experiences.
• Make time to listen to students formally and informally.
• Be interested in students as people as well as in their work.

- Initiate dialogue about what they find hard or easy about work and respond to their comments.
- Develop listening skills with students.

Development

Pollard (1997) offers an interesting analysis of the way teachers and children communicate in primary classrooms. He points out that in 1980, as part of the Oracle project, infant children spent 12 per cent of their day listening to and interacting with the teacher. At the time of the PACE project in 1994 this had risen to 40 per cent. In classrooms where Literacy and Numeracy Strategies dominate the curriculum, there is a good chance that the whole class teaching element has pushed this figure even higher. This means that it is very important that communication is successful in the whole class teaching phase of a lesson. It not only involves the teacher communicating clearly with the students, but also means that both teacher and students need to listen and respond. It is very common for the teacher to ask a question, a student to respond and then the teacher closes it down with an approving or disapproving remark. This is hardly the structure of genuine discussion and yet this question and answer routine is often claimed to be just that.

Pollard (1997) identifies four forms of listening: interactive, reactive, discriminative and appreciative. The interactive is the genuine discussion, the reactive a response to instruction, the discriminative a listening skill to distinguish sounds, and the appreciative where the listening is for enjoyment, such as hearing stories, music and poetry. What balance of these occur in your lessons?

Further reading

Pollard, A. (1997) *Reflective Teaching in the Primary School*, London: Cassell.

TTA Standards

1.2, 2.2.

Long-term planning

Long-term planning is the allocation of topics throughout the year for each subject. It is carried out in schools to ensure coverage of legal curricula (e.g. National Curriculum, DfEE, 2000). Planning in this way will ensure that students in different classes in the same year group get an equable programme and it should help with progression of the curriculum from year to year.

If long-term planning is not in place, then you need to consult with colleagues and subject/faculty leaders to establish what progression is expected. It is useful to outline your intentions for the year so that you can get a sense of pace and begin to allocate groups of lessons. At this point you will probably move on to medium-term planning. It will be likely that you can use the same long-term structure, with minor adjustments, the following year.

Links

Curriculum
Medium-term planning
Teaching in teams

Strategies

• Discuss long-term requirements with subject colleagues.
• Establish what you are required to cover throughout the year.
• Apportion the topics into half-term blocks.
• Use this outline to develop medium-term plans.

Development

Structured content varies enormously from country to country but there is remarkable similarity of goals in most curricula. An example of a very prescribed curriculum is that legally required in England, the National Curriculum, which has programmes of study for 5–16-year-olds and expected outcomes, attainment targets, arranged into ten levels of achievement. Additionally, at Key Stages 1, 2 and 3 (5 years to 14 years) there are tests to measure individual and school attainment. National qualifications are also in place. There is also strong guidance for teachers in the form of the *National Numeracy Strategy* (DfES, 1999) and the *National Literacy Strategy* (DfES, 1998) which leaves little room for variation in long-term planning. In secondary schools, the Key Stage 3 National Strategy will impact on long-term planning in all subject areas.

Coherent long-term planning is dependent on a whole school approach. This ensures a degree of progression for students. With a prescribed curriculum (as in the English National Curriculum) it is necessary to plan to include what is required for the year. Hopefully, this is reasonable in quantity, but at the same time has a breadth and balance of subjects. One suspects that there is always going to be more we would like to teach than we have time for. If the curriculum is not prescribed these decisions are made by the school or individual teachers.

Long-term planning is often a team activity, with subject teachers meeting and planning together. Some schools feel that provision should be totally equable across the year and insist that medium-term planning is shared and delivered at the same time (within the same week). This has the advantage of sharing the workload of planning but can be a challenge on resource provision.

Further reading

Department for Education and Employment (DfEE) (2000) *The National Curriculum*: Handbook for Primary Teachers in England Key Stages 1 and 2, London: DfEE/QCA (www.nc.uk.net).

Department for Education and Employment DfEE (2001a) *Key Stage 3 National Strategy Framework for Teaching Mathematics: Years 7, 8 and 9*, London: DfEE.

Department for Education and Employment DfEE (2001b) *Key Stage 3 National Strategy Framework for Teaching English: Years 7, 8 and 9*, London: DfEE.

Department for Education and Skills (DfES) (1998) *National Literacy Strategy*, London: DfES.

www.standards.dfes.gov.uk/keystage3

TTA Standards

2.1, 3.1.

Marking

Maybe we need to clearly establish why a piece of work is being marked. What purpose is your marking serving? Are the students clear about the purpose? As adults we seek others to 'mark' draft versions of documents and letters and we also possess our own checking strategies. There are sometimes opportunities to respond to the top copy, i.e. the final version, as well. If the top copy is marked then there is an expectation to carry forward marking advice to the next appropriate situation. There are differences between the adult world and the school world, so maybe we should be creating stronger links between school and adult writing situations. For teachers the following questions might arise:

Do students get an opportunity to draft work?
Do they get the final draft marked or the top copy?
How many top copies are expected and what is done with them?
What status in the work system does the exercise book have?
Do you write on the 'top copy'?

In school, marking work is a traditional response to providing feedback, often brought about by large classes generating work faster than the teacher can monitor it. It can form a written record of a student's progress. It is also a measure of end product. Grading is a way of marking which allows comparison with classmates or against set criteria. Comments can be encouraging and constructive. Teachers often wonder if students act upon written advice. Generally strategies are quite weak in ensuring students follow up the advice offered.

Consider also how useful the comments you make are going to be:

What effect do comments such as, 'See me' and 'Satisfactory' have on students?
Is 5/10 good, or did you expect everyone to gain 10/10?
How does this mark look when parents examine the books on parents' evening?
What sense will parents make of your comments? Sometimes the exercise books are the only evidence they see.

On draft work be positive, make comments which help students know what to do next. On final work, make comments positive, perceptive and praiseworthy. Try to mark with students present on some occasions, this means you can talk to them about the work. Students are keen to have feedback as soon as possible so try to have a quick turnaround on your marking. Allow time to address errors in a constructive way, maybe through discussion with peers or as a class. Encourage students to develop drafting and checking strategies.

You may wish to introduce an element of self-marking in some appropriate situations as this encourages students to seek their own feedback. It will be your responsibility to monitor these situations and get students to understand the significance of correct and incorrect answers. Competitive situations are difficult for students to deal with when self-marking.

Links

Active learning
Competition
Feedback
Formative assessment
Homework
Independent learning
Parents

Strategies

- Allow opportunities for students to respond to comments made by you (mark the final draft).
- Make comments encouraging with suggestions which students can act upon.
- Each half term, try to mark at least one piece of work with the student.
- Respond to problems quickly by talking about them if possible.
- Mark and return work by the next lesson whenever you can.
- Encourage self-editing and self-marking where appropriate.
- Encourage discussion about errors.
- Consider students producing work which they then use in class rather than have it marked.

Development

Marking is a practice which has been handed down almost as a tradition in teaching so maybe it is time to review the practice. A starting point for this might be to ask what purpose it serves in specific contexts. As a summative assessment response it has a clear function. As a formative assessment function there are situations where it may be better to provide alternative feedback of a constructive nature. If marking is used for formative purposes it needs to offer the student a way forward which they can act upon, such as, correcting a final draft rather than top copy. Systems of self-assessment may be a strategy you choose to introduce alongside your own marking.

Haydn (2001) offers advice on assessment and links this with accountability. Decisions on marking will eventually affect what outputs you select and how much time you allow to address feedback during lessons. You also need to be clear about your own marking strategies as you may be required to justify them to parents. Consider what messages they are getting from their children, their child's homework, their child's work on parents' evenings and from the school's official policies and communications with them.

Further reading

Haydn, T. (2001) Unit 6.1 'Assessment and accountability' in Capel, S., Leask, M. and Turner, T. (Eds) *Learning to Teach in Secondary Schools*, 3rd edn, London: Routledge.

Medium-term planning

This is the planning that takes place over a number of weeks. It draws upon the long-term planning or a syllabus. It is the stage where many teachers consider how they will teach an objective and what supporting activities they will require the students to carry out. They will also decide what resources they need to prepare or collect. Deciding on lessons which will generate good display material might be appropriate at this stage. Planning to include ICT and Key Skills will also be considered at the medium-term planning stage. It might be appropriate to differentiate at this stage. There is a balance of detail between the medium-term plans and the lesson plans depending on where you do your thinking about detail of delivery. It is possible that you opt to be well prepared in advance and then adjust your medium-term plans in the light of your lesson evaluations/students' performance.

There are examples of medium-term planning in the public domain. A good example is the QCA schemes of work, found at (www. teachernet.gov.uk).

Links

Differentiation
Lesson plan structure
Long-term planning
Resources

Strategies

- Draw upon long-term plans, curriculum documents and syllabi to establish the content of a block of work (e.g. half a term?).
- Consider objectives.

- Consider differentiation (and sub-objectives).
- Consider resources which need to be organized.
- Integrate the use of ICT and Key Skills.
- Plan for display work.

Development

Medium-term planning has similar issues to long-term planning strategies but some additional ones too. It is at this level that judgements are made about effective learning environments, teaching style and a variety of outputs from the students. Some of this is managing with what you have but there is some room to make choices and be inventive, to try out new approaches and instigate new systems of working with students.

Further reading

QCA schemes, examples of medium-term planning, can be found at www. teachernet.gov.uk

TTA Standards

3.1.2, 3.3.3.

Misconceptions and remedies

Students often misunderstand or develop their own rules for deciding how something should be done. This is part of normal development. Learning things correctly saves students from developing misconceptions. Sometimes students' *ad hoc* rules work in specific situations, but are not correct in others. You need to be clear and correct in what you teach and observant of students' responses. On discovering a misconception it needs to be unlearned and a correct procedure/fact learned. This is harder than learning correctly in the first place! It might be necessary to go back many steps to resolve the problems.

In lessons, if the misconception arises with the majority of the class when you are teaching them, it is best to stop everyone and go over the point again. If you discover a common misconception when marking homework, it is worth taking a few minutes to address the problem with the whole class in the next lesson. There are various strategies that teachers use to get students to address corrections. One possibility is to let students discuss errors with each other, under your general supervision. As a student works during the lesson, it may be necessary to intervene because you can see misconceptions or errors developing. It is useful to question the student at this point about his thinking. Often, on reflection, he will see his error and, if not, you still get some indication of how he is working something out which will enable you to give appropriate advice.

Errors and misconceptions are seen by students as mistakes and may be regarded by them as a sign of failure. In actuality, they are often signposts on the frontiers of understanding, and as such, indicate where new learning needs to take place. Putting misconceptions right should be given a positive spin with all your classes rather than be tucked away as, 'Five minutes to do your corrections before you go on to page twelve'.

Links

Active learning
Communicating clearly
Consolidation
Expectations about students' learning
Intellectual development
Lesson plan structure
Listening and responding to students

Strategies

- If a large number of students have not understood, stop the lesson and reiterate the point clearly.
- Allow time for students to discuss and correct errors.
- Plan time for discussion of mistakes and their causes.
- Question students about 'how' they have worked something out rather than launch into an early explanation.
- When marking, certain mistakes can indicate misconceptions which you then need to check with the student.

Development

Teacher subject knowledge is an important factor in preventing misconceptions. Before teaching a topic try to research the pedagogic knowledge you require. Initially this can be a large part of your planning load but becomes easier as you call upon your previous experience. Sometimes we fall back on what we were taught ourselves and may be unaware that we too have misconceptions. For example, it is not uncommon to say in mathematics, 'When you multiply two numbers the answer is bigger and when you divide the answer is smaller'. Consider the following:

$$\tfrac{1}{3} \times \tfrac{1}{3} = \tfrac{1}{9} \text{ (which is smaller)}$$

and then,

$$\tfrac{1}{3} \div \tfrac{1}{3} = \tfrac{3}{3} \text{ or } 1 \text{ (which is larger)}$$

This is a good example where the rule works with whole numbers but not when students start to extend the number system and deal with fractions. When discussing misconceptions try not to leave students without a way forward or with a solution to the problem.

Monitoring student learning

See *Formative assessment.*

More able students

See *Able students.*

Motivation

Finding ways of interesting your students in the learning you want them to do is an excellent idea. Helping them to behave in acceptable ways so they can learn is also important. The learner's motivation is a key to this.

Some students want to learn. Others are less keen! Some students expect to do well. Some are sure that they won't be able to do well. Some learners think that they are successful because they are lucky, others think it is because they work hard, others because they are clever. This helps to explain why some students of similar ability achieve more than others.

Motivation is also to do with what individuals *expect* and *want* from the activity you've set. The student's reason for choosing, doing (performing), and keeping at (persisting) the tasks you set will vary.

Motivating students to learn is clearly a major preoccupation for teachers. You'll recognize that some students have *intrinsic motivation* that comes from internal sources such as curiosity, interest, pleasure, an innate need for mastery and growth. These students feel some sense of control over themselves. They are often concerned with the task rather than worrying about what others think about them. Others work better for rewards, known as a form of *extrinsic motivation*, as it comes from an external source. These students want to succeed perhaps to avoid punishment, or for a high mark, or to please others. For most people both systems operate at the same time.

Maslow (1970) suggested that there is a *hierarchy of needs* that has to be satisfied for people to do well. He suggests that lower order needs like having sufficient sleep and food and being loved have to be met before learning can take place as learning is a higher order need. An example of this in school might be students not learning because they are tired, hungry or frightened.

Links

Motivation is a key topic in these links:

Active learning
Competition
Differentiation
Discipline
Expectations about students' learning
Independent learning
Learning styles
Listening and responding to pupils
Purposeful working atmosphere
Research and its uses
Rewards
Target setting

Strategies

- Your students need to feel valued. Aim for your lessons to be low on criticism and high on warmth (empathy). You and the students have to celebrate achievement and limit blame.
- Emphasize personal judgement about personal capabilities to encourage students to think of their *successes as due to high ability* and attribute *lack of success to lack of effort*. Phrases like, 'You've worked hard' rewards effort; 'You're clever at that now' confirms ability.

- Each student you teach needs to believe that he/she can succeed through effort. This means that you have to set tasks that enable success but require effort.

Development

In Behaviourist theory the emphasis is on managing the learning situation with incentives and reinforcements built in. This standpoint suggests that inner thoughts, feelings or psychological needs are not important, indeed they need not be considered for effective learning to occur. This is often the approach you'll use. Your use of rewards will include, for example house points, or extra time on the computer, while punishments include loss of privilege. Cognitive theorists, on the other hand, see motivation as a crucial element in learning. The strategies listed here start to deal with aspects of motivation. Motivation is to do with the judgements anyone makes about his/her ability to succeed at a task. This evaluation is informed by what happened in the past, the models that friends supply (think of peer pressure) and the feedback we get from others.

Further reading

Bigge, M. L. and Shermis, S. S. (1998) *Learning Theories for Teachers*, 6th edn, New York: Addison Wesley Longman. A thorough review of the important theories on motivation.

Maslow, A. (1970) *Motivation and Personality*, 2nd edn, New York: Van Nostrand.

TTA Standard

3.3.3.

National qualifications

The English 14–19 curriculum (KS4/5) is assessed through national qualifications. The national framework allows for general and vocationally related and occupational qualifications, starting with certification in school, but moving into the workplace and further and higher education at 18 plus and beyond. Students have choices to make at 14 about the routes they can take. Blurring the distinctions between academic, vocational and occupational qualification is by no means new. This is the latest attempt. From now on, the main emphasis will be giving a greater variety of qualifications and giving parity between them. Many students will take a mixture of academic and vocational subjects or vocational and occupational qualifications. In England, whilst children can leave school at 16 years, it is government policy to encourage students to stay on for another two years. This is all part of a strategy to develop 'life-long learners'. Each of the named certificates has a level number and each is further classified as foundation, intermediate or advanced level.

At 16 the traditional academic route is to take the *General Certificates of Secondary Education* (GCSE), public examinations with limited teacher assessment in the subjects for which they are entered. In the national framework these are general qualifications. These will be level 1, (foundation level) for grades D–G and level 2 (intermediate level) for grades C–A*. This is followed by a further two years of study with fewer subjects taken at AS/A level. Often students will specialize in either arts or sciences at this stage. In the national framework, these are level 3, advanced level study.

General National Vocational Qualifications (GNVQs), soon to be renamed *Applied GCSE*, offers an alternative route. As for GCSE, students study for two years; their work is generally teacher assessed through portfolios, rather than by examination. These are vocationally related areas of study, e.g. media, engineering, or social studies. A merit in a GNVQ is equivalent to 2 Grade C passes at GCSE. In the national framework this would be level 2 intermediate level. Advanced level GNVQs are vocational A levels. In the national framework, these are level 3, advanced level.

Some school students will follow occupational qualifications, specific job related skills, e.g. bricklaying, hairdressing or child care, will be taught, often in the work place, to gain *National Vocational Qualifications* (NVQs) at levels 1–3. (NVQ levels 4 and 5 are gained after leaving school.) In the national framework NVQs have the following levels:

- *Foundation*, level 1, these are equivalent to GCSE grade D–G and Foundation GNVQ.
- *Intermediate*, level 2, these are equivalent to GCSE grade C–A* and Intermediate GNVQ.

---

*These are often taken in all the subjects the student has followed from entry to secondary school.

- *Advanced,* level 3, these are equivalent to A level and Vocational A level.

In the national qualifications' framework there is also an entry level which will enable students to gain a *Certificate of (Educational) Achievement.* For most school students these will probably be in work related learning i.e. Key and Core Skills.

Links
Curriculum.

Further reading

QCA (2000) *Finding Your Way Around: A Leaflet About the National Qualifications Framework,* London: QCA, is an excellent starting place.
Gill, P. and Johnson, S. (2001) '14–19 education: broadening the curriculum' in Dillon, J. and Maguire, M. (Eds) *Becoming a Teacher: Issues in Secondary Teaching,* 2nd edn, Buckingham: Open University, pp. 273–83, offers a thoughtful critique on this aspect of the curriculum.

TTA Standard
2.3.

Out-of-school learning opportunities

Well thought through learning outcomes will be part of the preparation for the planned activity but there will be other benefits which cannot always be specified. Students learn different things beyond the classroom. They may grow in self confidence, develop an interest, or discover something else about themselves. Visits, part of a day, or longer, locally, or further afield, can increase a student's competence and independence as a learner. They add an extra dimension to learning that is difficult to achieve in school.

To make the most, educationally, of a visit you will need to prepare the students beforehand so that they can make sense of what they see. Usually visits are linked to the curriculum, they complement the work going on in the lessons.

During the visit you may ask students to look out for particular objects or events. If you have too much paperwork they will spend their time desperately trying to fill in the answers. This will mean that they miss much of what is going on. Think carefully about exactly what you want them to gain from the visit and then plan accordingly.

For example, you might want Year 7 students to write about what it is like to live in an Iron Age round house, having visited the reconstruction where there is a speaker, it would be appropriate for the students to make notes from the talk. You may then ask them to make a list of adjectival phrases whilst they observe the surroundings and feel the atmosphere.

On returning to school you should allow time for follow-up work. This work could vary in form from drama to displays, booklets, imaginative writing or scientific experiment, whatever is most appropriate for your subject.

The benefits of taking students on visits greatly outweigh the risks. You will be expected to assess the hazards and make sure that they are going to be reasonably safe. You are advised to read the link in this book on *Safety* which summarizes some of the actions you should take. There will be specific considerations about hazards and risks for particular out-of-school learning. Embarking on visits and activities beyond school means planning for the worst but expecting the best. You will want to leave nothing to chance. Parents will need sufficient information to be able to make informed choices associated with the out-of-school learning opportunity. They will need information on the learning benefits and the possible risks; and about the actions in place to ensure risks are minimized.

As far as you can you will want to ensure that all students can have the opportunity to go. This will mean that the visit is suitable and accessible to all. Extra expense is a huge burden for some parents. Some students have special needs, medical conditions, cultural or religious requirements that need to be accounted for in setting up the activity. The decision is fairly easy to make where you have a well disciplined group; out-of-school learning activities ought to happen. Sometimes you will need to make a hard decision to deny a student the chance to accompany the group because his or her behaviour is likely to be unreliable. In these cases you need to ensure that this aspect of the curriculum is provided in other ways.

Links

Curriculum
Discipline
Expectations about students' learning
Long-term planning

Medium-term planning
Safety

Strategies

All these factors need to be considered:

- Include visits in long- and medium-term planning.
- Build in appropriate preparation and follow-up work.
- Get permission from necessary authorities, including parents.
- Book visit, guides, speakers and transport.
- Organize adult supervision and check health and safety factors including completion of risk assessment.
- Inform parents and students, of schedule and food, money and clothing requirements.
- Have a great day!

Development

Any learning that takes place away from school should be considered as out-of-school learning. Students only spend a few hours each day in school, the rest of the time their learning continues beyond the school gates. Out-of-school learning is more than the visits and opportunities you will plan as part of the curriculum. Much out-of-school learning will be unplanned, a natural consequence of being part of a family and a community. Home influences on younger children have been much studied, as they are clearly important. The home continues to be important as children develop into young adulthood: attitudes, aspirations and opportunities are often family driven. The added dimension of increased independence means that friends, part-time work and leisure activities become part of the learning experience.

Further reading

Desforges, C. (1995) 'Learning out of school' in Desforges, C. (Ed.) *An Introduction to Teaching*, Oxford: Blackwell. This chapter surveys research about home and community learning.

www.baalpe.org This is a good example of a specific subject site. The British Association of Advisers and Lecturers in PE has definitive information on Safe Practice in Physical Education. This can be used to make safe practice guidelines for other subjects.

www.teachernet.gov.uk/visits This site sets out good practice for health and safety on visits.

TAA Standard

3.1.5.

Pace

The right pace is when you have students' attention, as learning is most likely to take place when you have their attention. Getting the pace of a lesson right is challenging because students learn at different rates. In oral sessions you will be trying to work at a speed which engages your more able students but also allows the rest of the class to understand, including those who learn more slowly. This can be thought of as communicating at several levels through the language you use, the content of the work and the general class and individual questions you ask.

If your explanations are too long or you ask too many questions which require explanatory answers, you risk lowering the overall pace. As the pace slows some students stop paying attention, some will day-dream and some may begin to misbehave. If the pace is too fast some students fail to comprehend the teaching points and are unable to complete follow-up tasks. Either way, learning has not taken place.

Poor behaviour can lead to the teacher engaging in one-to-one discipline talks which further slows the pace of the lesson. Also while you engage with one student, the behaviour of other students can begin to deteriorate. Deal quickly with behaviour problems or sort them out at the end of the session. Better still, try and anticipate them and have strategies to forestall them. (For example, have a seating plan that gives you direct access to students who may misbehave or move through the room so that you are near students who show signs of restlessness or inattention.)

When students are doing tasks, pace is important too. It is useful to give them completion times and targets to remind them of this during the task period. For example, 'You should have answered at least three questions by now' and 'You have ten minutes left so begin to check your work'. Students need to learn to stay on task so make this a clear expectation. Differentiation is important because this allows the task to be manageable.

Links

Communication about learning
Completed work

Differentiation
Discipline
Motivation
Questioning

Strategies

- Raise the pace if students are restless. Lower the pace if you want to give students time to think.
- Use strategies to maintain pace in whole class teaching situations.
- Extend or shorten oral sessions depending on whether the students are engaged in the work.
- Use a mixture of questions that elicit long and short answers.
- Differentiate questions and content to include the range of ability of the class in oral sessions and group tasks.
- In whole class sessions decide when it is time to move on (as students begin to disengage).
- Convey expectations about completion of work and time available.
- Check through the lesson that you are maintaining your timing (only change this if you can justify it to yourself).
- Avoid lengthy one-to-ones about misbehaviour in whole class situations (anticipate, then deal with quickly or later).

Development

The Hay McBer report (2000, 1.2.9) states, 'Effective teachers achieve the management of the class by having a clear structure for each lesson, making full use of planned time, using a brisk pace and allocating his/her time fairly amongst pupils'. Getting the pace right by being sensitive as to how the students are responding, and being well organized will go a long way to ensuring the they are on task for a high percentage of your lesson.

Kounin (1970) observed teachers communicating with their classes and found four types of action that teachers took which disrupted the flow of their lessons. He described these as dangles, flip flops, overdwelling and fragmentation.

The dangles left the delivery unfinished.
The flip flop was a change of subject mid-sentence.
The overdwelling was spending too long on a topic already grasped by the students.

The fragmentation was splitting up the work into so many small steps that the students lost the purpose of the lesson.

The general impetus is to increase the pace to ensure students' attention and reasonable behaviour. It is worth considering whether the pace matches the task. It would be quite easy for students to abdicate from higher order thinking when the teacher moves on too quickly and does not allow enough time to work something out.

Further reading

Kounin, J. (1970) *Discipline and Group Management in the Classroom*, New York: Holt Reinhart and Winston.

Hay McBer (2000) *Research into Teacher Effectiveness: A Model of Teacher Effectiveness*, London: DfEE www.dfes.gov.uk/teachingreforms/leadership/mcber/.

Pollard, A and Twigg, P. (1997) *The Reflective Teacher in the Secondary School*, London: Cassell Chapter 10 on lesson planning provides further practical advice.

TTA Standard

3.3.7.

Parents

Parents, the people who care for the students in your classes, have rights and responsibilities. Your respect for them is central to establishing and maintaining a working relationship.

Who are parents?

This depends on the circumstances. The child's natural parent(s) may not always be the person/people with responsibility. Step-parents, relatives, co-habitees of step-parents and relatives and adoptive parents may all take on parental responsibility. In the UK, foster carers and people employed by Local Education Authorities to care for children subject to residence orders or care orders are not treated in the same way by Education Acts, but in practical terms will often be treated by school authorities as taking parental responsibility.

What is parental responsibility?

These are all the rights, duties, powers, responsibilities which a parent of a child has by law. For example, in the UK it is a parental responsibility to ensure that school-aged children attend school.

What is parenting style?

The way that students are dealt with at home will make a difference to their response to teachers and peers. Some parents are very strict and controlling: they adopt an authoritarian style. This may mean that children have too little freedom to develop. Some give children opportunities to make mistakes and support their development in many ways – this authoritative style enables development. Others give in to the child's whim: an indulgent style. Some seem not to care to deal with their child's growth: an uninvolved style.

Links

Communication with parents
Teachers' employment and conditions

TTA Standard

1.4.

Physical development

Factors such as cultural practices, nutrition and experiences all influence growth and development. Heredity is likely to determine eventual height and physical appearance. This helps to account for the considerable physical differences you'll see between students of the same age.

Human growth is comparatively slow. It is not until between a year and fourteen months that most children can walk unaided. Physical development is at its most rapid in infancy, children get taller and stronger more rapidly between 0–5 years. Growth slows from about 6 until the onset of puberty. Until puberty differences in height, weight and muscle mass between girls and boys are slight, for example, both sexes can be expected to have a similar ability to run and jump.

The onset of puberty brings changes in the sexual characteristics. It is worth knowing about this as the psychological effects are considerable for some adolescents. Parents and students are often suprisingly ill-informed about the changes that take place. As a teacher you are often well placed to give accurate information to your students. As there are legal constraints on what you can teach you should do this within the guidelines provided by your school. Physical development at this stage is complex. There are changes in the reproductive system, in the cardio-vascular system and the lungs with an affect on the respiration system and the size and strength of many muscles in the body. Often there is a 'growth spurt'; some youngsters grow very tall really fast. The variation between the onset of puberty and the rate of growth between individuals is considerable. You'll have students of the same age who are young men and women, working alongside others who are still children. Although this is perfectly normal it can be a source of considerable anxiety both to adolescents and their parents. The growth spurt may start as young as 9 for some boys, but may not happen until 15. While girls may start as young as 7 or 8, but may not until they are 12, 13 or 14. The average, though, for boys is around 12 and between 10–11 for girls.

Links

Adolescence
Emotional development
Intellectual development
Linguistic development
Social development

Further reading

Turner, T. (2001) 'Unit 4.2 Growth, development and diet' in Capel, S., Leask, M. and Turner, T. (2001) *Learning to Teach in Secondary Schools*, 3rd edn, London: Routledge, pp. 147–59 is a useful introduction.
Head, J. (2001) 'Adolescence' in Dillon, J. and Maguire, M. (Eds) *Becoming a Teacher: Issues in Secondary Teaching*, Buckingham: Open University Press, pp. 136–41 is also useful.

TTA Standard

2.4.

Problem solving

Life is full of problems that need to be solved therefore this is a process which needs to be present in education. Much has been written about the skills and processes involved in problem solving in different subjects. Whether you see it as a way into new work or as an opportunity to apply acquired knowledge, it is an essential life skill and a rationale for gaining new skills and knowledge (using what you learn).

Sometimes teachers provide students with problems and investigations for which the children fail to get started or do not come up with a solution. As in real life, no-one can immediately solve all problems. Often time is needed to try different strategies or make a useful mental link or acquire new relevant knowledge. What students do need is knowledge of the strategies or processes which can be used to try and solve problems. These need to be overtly taught just like the rest of the curriculum. In your subject getting started, sorting the data, seeking patterns, linking to what you know, trying out a theory, testing a theory, etc. are all ways of working which you have to help students understand and use.

Links

Active learning
Explaining
Group work
Independent learning
Intervention
Listening and responding to pupils
Skills and strategies
Thinking skills

Strategies

- Include problem solving in medium-term planning in suitable lessons.
- Help students with processes by teaching and discussing them, make these lesson objectives.
- Do 'whole class' problem solving to start with to demonstrate the thinking processes they need to use.
- Use problem solving to consolidate work and to assess whether students have a working knowledge of a piece of learning.
- Or, use a problem to introduce a topic and engage interest.
- Develop a range of verbal 'prompts' to help students think about their work when they are stuck (which can be in the form of a set of questions).

- Reassure students that work often leads to 'dead ends' and that they sometimes need to go back and pick up a new thread.

Development

You can set problems that have a single step and one solution for example, in Art, 'Which two paints do you mix to create orange?'. Other problems have many steps before you arrive at the solution. A common error that students make is to find a solution but not check back to see if it answers the original question. For example, a student who says that, '3.4 children can go in each minibus for the trip to the swimming pool'. A further set of problems are those that are open ended. Sometimes these open-ended problems are known as investigations. They also offer the opportunity for students to make decisions and pose questions. There are opportunities within them to decide which lines of enquiry you will pursue. Students may have different solutions and even more questions in this type of enquiry. All these forms of work require students to develop a process of tackling problems which brings together use of their prior knowledge and generic strategies for what to do next. Fisher (1987) writes about the processes primary school children employ in problem solving. His strategies are in the form of a series of child-friendly questions. These questions are useful for younger secondary students too. Muijs *et al.* (2001) provide a theoretical perspective for this aspect of teaching.

Further reading

De Bono, E. (1969) *Thought and Thinking (The Five Day Course in Thinking)*, London: Penguin.
Burton, L. (1984) *Thinking Things Through*, Oxford: Blackwell.
Fisher, R. (1987) *Problem Solving in the Primary School*, Oxford: Blackwell.
Muijs, D. and Reynolds, D. (2001) *Effective Teaching: Evidence and Practice*, London: Paul Chapman.

Purposeful working atmosphere

It is important to have a purposeful working atmosphere because it is in this environment that learning is most likely to take place. There is also the implication that students will be engaged in work they see as meaningful and are therefore motivated to do. Lots of factors come together to create this kind of environment. A purposeful working atmosphere is often observed in classrooms where the teachers believe that students should be independent learners: it appears that it is more likely to be achieved if the students see the work as their work, and not something that is totally imposed by the teacher. Others would argue that this is not true and it is purely a matter of clarity of purpose and good organization.

Whichever view you hold, to move towards achieving a purposeful working atmosphere it is important that all the students understand what they are working towards and that the work is at a level in which they can engage and contribute. This will assist in helping them to stay on task. It is the teacher's responsibility to motivate the students to complete the task and complete it well. The teacher must make it clear what standard of work, behaviour and style of working they expect in their lessons. This is often done quite overtly when the teacher first begins to work with the class and is gently reinforced over a period of time.

Links

Communication about learning
Discipline
Equal opportunities
Expectations about students' learning
Listening and responding to pupils
Motivation
Relationships with pupils
Target setting

Strategies

- Clear expectations of how the students are going to go about the work.
- Well differentiated work (lesson planning and formative assessment).
- Attainable and clearly stated objectives, shared with the students.
- Generate an enthusiasm in the students to do the work (motivation).
- Well organized resources.
- Encourage students to take responsibility through decision making about their own work.

Development

Underpinning a purposeful working environment will be a well established relationship between the teacher and the students. The students sense that the teacher is interested in what they are doing and know the rules of conduct and work procedures in the class. In return, the teacher provides a stimulating environment, fairness of action and a genuine interest in the work and welfare of the students.

Physically, the classroom, the students' working space and yours, should be clean, tidy and warm, with stimulating display material. Students will want to be there. They may even have a sense of ownership and contribute to the maintenance and development of the teaching space, and might volunteer their time to do this.

The teacher will also ensure that the work environment is non-threatening. It will be a place where students feel that they are able to contribute, even if it only is a tentative suggestion. There will be no fear that they are going to be ridiculed by their peers or rejected by the teacher.

TTA Standards

2.7, 3.2.4, 3.3.8.

Questioning

There are several different types of questioning which elicit different forms of response from students. The most common form of questioning observed in the classroom is: teacher asks question, student gives short response, teacher gives a short response indicating whether she or he approves of the answer or thinks it is wrong. This closed questioning is designed to get a simple, often anticipated response, for example, 'What is the capital of France?' and, 'What is 9×7?'.

Open questions are those where students might offer any one of a range of answers or explanations. For example, 'How could you work that out?' or, 'What do you think happened next in the sequence of events?'. Open questions promote students' articulation of their thinking.

Students are very good at working out whether they have given a successful answer. They read the teacher's body language and interpret the teacher's responses. For example, if a teacher frowns slightly or says 'Are you sure?', they will assume they have given a wrong answer and will often offer an alternative response. However, the teacher's intention in asking, 'Are you sure?' might be asking the pupil to justify his or her response. Your students, however, quickly get used to the pattern of your questioning.

When students are struggling, sometimes it is a better strategy to question what they have done so far or suggest a way forward. These are 'prompt' questions and help students to articulate their thinking. Often this allows a student to see a way forward for themselves.

As you work with your students you should increasingly expect them to justify their responses.

Links

Active learning
Communication about learning
Demonstration by the teacher
Explaining
Feedback
Independent learning
Instruction
Intervention
Listening and responding to students
Pace
Thinking skills
Whole class teaching

Strategies

- Use a range of question types.
- When you want to increase the pace of an oral session use closed questions.
- When you want to explore students' thinking and encourage their explanations, use more open questions.
- To promote consolidation of understanding ask children to talk about what they have done.
- If a child is stuck, use a 'prompt' question.
- Experiment with the balance between your information giving and your questioning.
- Increase the level of demand for able students.
- As you work with the class, increasingly expect them to justify their responses (e.g. use 'Why?' as a follow up question).

Development

Pollard and Trigg (1995: 321–5) have a useful framework for self-analysis of this aspect of your work. They suggest an analysis of questioning in whole class oral situations and offer strategies for use of different types of questioning, including higher order questions which are aimed at eliciting responses which require pupils to think. Such questions might require them to analyse information, offer informed opinion or make new links between known facts.

It is very much the teacher's responsibility to create a classroom environment where it is alright to ask questions. It is very easy to misuse questions about work in order to discipline poor behaviour or inattentiveness. This leads to a reluctance to answer academic questions, so make behaviour questions/statements clearly about behaviour only.

Further reading

Brown, G. and Wragg, E. (1993) *Questioning*, London: Routledge.
Pollard, A. and Trigg, P. (1997) *The Reflective Teacher in the Secondary School*, London: Continuum.

TTA Standard

3.3.3.

Recording individual progress

When considering what you are going to record, always be clear about the purpose, as this will help you identify what is most useful to collect evidence about (assessment criteria).

Recording individual progress happens at various levels and for different purposes. In your lessons you will probably wish to keep detailed 'informal notes' about students meeting specific objectives or having difficulty. This is done to enable you to keep track of how each student is progressing. These 'notes' will feed into your lesson planning and could be used to inform a more official record.

At the next level there will be particular information which needs to be passed on to others such as the SENCO (Special Educational Needs Co-ordinator), the next form tutor, parents, school records and other agencies, such as Connexions. Schools often decide the nature of the information they wish to send or receive.

A third level is official and legal. There are requirements to report on individual progress to parents and Local Education Authorities (LEAs). In England there are also legal requirements for information on annual reports to parents (see *Communicating with parents*) and teacher assessment within the key stage assessment procedures (see *Summative assessment*).

Links

Formative assessment
Marking
Parents
Special Educational Needs
Summative assessment
Target setting

Strategies

- Before teaching decide what assessment system you will run.
- Before teaching devise appropriate recording formats.
- Choose manageable assessment criteria and ones that will inform you about students' understanding.
- Check what information needs to be collected over the long-term (half-term, term, year) including information needed for national qualifications. Devise a strategy to ensure that you can acquire this evidence.
- Build into your planning a strategy to deal with the findings of your assessments (i.e. when will you deal with individuals who do not understand this work; day-to-day, week-to-week, medium-term?).

Development

For a student teacher recording serves several purposes. One purpose is to track individuals and inform the subject teachers of individual student progress at the end of the practice. Another is to ensure that you develop assessment procedures as part of the teaching cycle. Your recording will provide evidence, for both you and your mentor, of how consistent you are in collecting information about individuals and how you use that information. Another purpose is that teaching practice is the place where you are given the opportunity to practise a variety of assessment and recording methods, which you will need as a qualified teacher. This includes those records on which you will need to make judgements for external purposes such as National Qualifications. For teachers who spend a complete year working with classes, their recording is more likely to be done in the medium-term. They also have a wealth of experience against which to measure those who lie outside the normal range of progress. As a beginner it is worth noting how this is done.

Further reading

Capel, S. Leask, M. and Turner, T. (2001) *Learning to Teach in Secondary Schools*, 3rd edn, London: Routledge.
Pollard, A. and Trigg, P. (1997) *The Reflective Teacher in the Secondary School*, London: Continuum.

TTA Standard

3.2.7.

Relationships with students

The way that you work with your students, what you say to them, how you treat them and the respect you show them, help to build your reputation. If you think back to your own school days you will recall the teachers you liked and those you disliked. As well as expecting you to teach them your subject, your students expect other things from you. Beyond achievement in the subject, they do want you to:

be approachable;
take an interest in them;
want to know about them as people.

Many adolescents have deep concerns about serious issues. They want to be able to talk to you about the things that matter to them. They don't expect you to treat everyone in exactly the same way, but they do expect to be treated fairly. Your students value firmness, for example, they think that you should enforce school rules.

Your personal code of conduct will be based on your understanding of ethical principles, legal requirements, contract of employment, the job and role and the expectations other colleagues, parents and the community beyond the school have. There are some things that are never acceptable, for example, a sexual liaison with someone you teach, advocating illegal acts, or promoting a particular political party. You should be cautious about any meetings with any student on a one to one basis. This is not to say that these should never happen, just that it would be naïve not to safeguard your good name.

Links

Bullying
Child protection
Emotional development
Equal opportunities
Inclusion
Learning environment
Motivation
Social development
Teachers' employment and conditions
Values and ethos

Strategies

Recognize that students have expectations about you, which are based on previous experience of teachers and on your subject. If, in the past, these were on the whole good, you're on a winner. All you have to do is teach well and treat them fairly. If past experience of teachers and your subject was poor, then your task will be much harder. In either case:

- Take account of learners' feelings and emotions about your subject. What are their anxieties? How motivated are they?
- Share your excitement and enthusiasm for your subject.
- Respect your students by preparing to meet their different needs. Accept their standards, either high or low, as a starting place for better things.
- On individual basis, praise effort (persistence) and celebrate achievement.
- Set able students higher targets.
- Relate feedback to learning objectives.
- Be aware of your own views about race, gender, class and special needs, and how these will be recognized and understood by those you teach.

- Make sure that you treat students fairly by sharing out your time fairly.
- Avoid remarks that may be received as negative. Be careful that your jokes are not at someone's expense.
- Be approachable, teaching is a two-way process; students can ask questions to make things clearer, while teachers need to give feedback.
- Be yourself, teaching does use acting skills, but students very soon know more about you than you often know yourself.

Development

Sometimes the way we are required to deal with students conflicts with our personal set of values. For example, you may not care about whether a student is in school uniform or not, but in your school you're expected to enforce the school dress code. If there is a mismatch between your views and school policy you must seek to make your case at policy level, i.e. with the school leaders, not at student level. It is worth thinking through how to deal with this. It certainly seems that the more we are task involved – focused on actions – and the less ego involved – worried about how what we do makes us feel – the easier it is to live with some of the inconsistencies that being a teacher involves.

Further reading

Capel, S., Leask, M. and Turner, T. (2001) *Learning to Teach in Secondary Schools*, 3rd edn, London: Routledge. Section 1 has a wealth of advice.

Cowley, S. (1999) *Starting Teaching: How to Succeed and Survive*, London: Continuum.

Thody, A., Gray, B. and Bowden, D. (2000) *The Teacher's Survival Guide*, London: Continuum.

TTA Standard

3.3.1.

Research and its uses

'What research questions should I be asking?' 'What's worth spending precious time on?' Research questions can arise from what you do in your teaching, through questioning your own knowledge about the content of your subject. You will want to find out why some of your teaching is more effective, some less so, and more about the ways in which students learn best. In your school, you might ask, 'What are the best solutions to the challenges here?' Beyond the school you need to know about current issues so that you can question these. Furthermore, it is a proper and a legitimate use of your time. In England research is a Teacher Training Agency (TTA) standard for teachers. It is also part of the General Teaching Council's professional code. For your own professionalism it is important for you to be a learner, risk taker and an explorer, after all, this is what we ask school students to do. Research for teachers has several aspects: it supports subject knowledge, how we teach (pedagogy); and also addresses wider issues in education.

Knowledge about the subjects you teach needs to be kept up-to-date. From time to time curriculum development means that you will need to learn something new. You need to know what students may find hard to learn so that you can pay extra attention to making this as easy as possible for them. To do this you'll research subjects thoroughly; you'll make sure that what you are teaching is accurate.

You will want to know that the way you teach is as effective as possible and your reflections about the relationships between teaching and learning will lead you into doing research on the subject, in order to be more knowledgeable about it. You will want students to look forward to your lessons, even when the ideas are difficult. At first you may plan some of your teaching following ideas that work for other teachers. With experience your repertoire of teaching approaches will expand. The research question is, 'What works for me?'. You will want to put yourself in a strong position to argue for your approach. You will be basing your teaching on something other than a hunch, or 'it works because it works'. Your research will take the form of assessing the effectiveness of your actions through the evidence you collect from learning in your own classroom.

Keeping yourself informed about issues beyond the classroom means that you will know what policies are likely to impact on your work. An international perspective is important as well. Reading the education press and professional journals alerts you to the world beyond the classroom. This will often inform your reflection on your own practice. Your information will also be used in discussions with colleagues.

Links

Active learning
Continuing professional development
Independent learning
Teachers' employment and conditions

Strategies

- Question your own ways of knowing through reading, networking and keeping up-to-date on issues.
- Read the research:
    read critically and find alternative views to make the most of research;
    survey the literature by reading the summaries rather than whole articles;
    use databases, for example British Educational Index (BEI) and Educational Resources Information Centre (ERIC), to locate the areas that interest you;
    carry out searches for particular information through search engines like www.google.com; be aware that the WWW has both splendidly authoritative sources and the most awful rubbish available on it, with all shades in between.
- Network with others who are interested in similar areas through local professional groups, local university contacts and national and international associations.
- In the UK use the websites of official bodies such as the TTA, Department for Education and Skills (DfES), Office for Standards in Education (Ofsted), Qualifications and Curriculum Agency and British Educational Communications and Technology Agency (BECTa) to identify the issues that they think important. These bodies are policy makers so the research they support and commission is often related to a particular view.
- Use university and teacher centre libraries and librarians to get to the best research.
- Seek sponsorship for classroom enquiry and continuing professional development (e.g. DfES, TTA, Education Action Zones all offer opportunities for funding).

Development

As you teach you will be thinking about the research you have read and making connections with your work. You may well start to develop an interest in a particular aspect of teaching. At that point you will want to ask your own research questions. When you are ready to carry out some research of your own, training and support for research is offered by universities. You may be able to fund this through your school's staff development fund, or through grants made for this purpose from a variety of sources. Teachers who choose to research practice often find it time consuming; they also admit that the challenge was worthwhile and invigorating.

Further reading

Banks, F. and Shelton Mayes, A. (Eds) (2001) *Early Professional Development for Teachers*, London: Open University/David Fulton. Section 3 has an interesting selection of articles about research.

Matherson, C. and Matherson, D. (Eds) (2000) *Educational Issues in the Learning Age*, London: Continuum.

Pring, R. (2000) *Philosophy of Education Research*, London: Continuum.

Sayer, J. (2000) *The General Teaching Council*, London: Continuum.

Scott Baumann, A., Bloomfield, A. and Roughton, L. (Eds) (1997) *Becoming a Secondary Teacher*, London: Hodder & Stoughton Educational. Chapters 1, 9 and 31 are excellent introductions to both the issues and actions you may wish to take.

www.DfES.uk.gov lists Best Practice Research Scholarships sponsored by TTA.

www.teachernet.gov.uk outlines current DfES commissioned research.

Some commissioned research is reported on these sites as well:

www.canteach.gov.uk

www.curriculumonline.gov.uk

www.ofsted.gov.uk

www.becta.org.uk

www.qca.org.uk

TTA Standard

1.7.

Resources

Good resources can provide a stimulating start to a lesson as well as offering useful visual images (a picture is worth a thousand words?). Well-resourced practical work enhances the learning environment because students are able to work in a physical as well as a mental medium.

There are two kinds of resources; those that are readily available for your lessons and those that you have to acquire or make. This second group need to be considered when you do your medium-term planning to allow you time to assemble them. The second group of resources might include, posters, a range of materials, a set of demonstration cards, a collection of artefacts from a historical period or books and videos for a particular topic.

When you are considering the resources you are going to use, take into account social, cultural and gender implications, and ensure that you provide a fair curriculum for your students. Schools are not wealthy and sometimes resources such as books can be quite old. Check that the textbooks you use are appropriate for students growing up in this day and age. It is part of your role as a teacher to ensure that you monitor the resources available to students in your lessons.

Links

Culture
Differentiation
Equal opportunities
Formative assessment
Purposeful working atmosphere
Social development

Strategies

- Plan at medium-term level for resources you need to make or acquire.
- Try and find resources that illustrate well the teaching points you are going to make.
- Create a visually stimulating environment (interactive too).
- Use a variety of resources to capture attention.
- Use resources to bring the outside world into the lessons (real examples related to your subject).
- Update and check that your resources are appropriate for modern society.

Development

Unfortunately, schools never seem to have quite enough money to buy all the resources they would like. Many teachers are ingenious at making their own resources. These are often the most effective too, because the teacher knows what is appropriate for his or her students and what is going to be effective in illustrating what he or she wants to teach. Good ideas for teachers are now abundant on websites as well as in books. When planning to use resources, make sure that they are prepared, so time is not wasted in lessons. When planning to use resources select those which support the learning that you expect to take place. Occasionally resources can be used as an open-ended stimulus. Sometimes students bring ideas and artefacts into the classroom which can be opportunities for spontaneous learning.

When developing independent learning there will be times when you expect students to make decisions about what resources they think are going to help them carry out a task.

How are your resources organized?
Are they accessible?
Do students need to ask you for everything or are certain things openly available?
How do you organize for resources to be kept tidy?
Is tidiness an expectation of every individual or do you have monitors?
If you have monitors does this mean students can leave things out because they know others will 'clear up'?

Think through the implications of your organization.

Further reading
An example of a teacher's resource site on the web can be found at:
www.ambleside.schoolzone.co.uk/flashindex.htm an award winning primary school site.
www.curriculumonline.gov.uk for digital learning materials.

TTA Standards
3.3.1, 3.3.8.

Rewards

Do not undervalue the power of positive comment. As human beings we respond to praise and encouragement. The need to be 'overt' with younger students, sometimes this feels excessive but, as long as the student's action is worthy of praise, be unstinting with it. Praise does wonders for students' confidence and motivation. It is a challenge in any lesson to avoid being negative. When only positive comments are heard aloud it has the effect of creating a positive environment where students are happy to work.

As students get older, praising remarks have to be more subtle in both what you say and where and when it is said. These students still need the feedback that you will give. They also need to know what they have got right. But they will be more concerned about their status with their peers than teachers' approval. This peer pressure can also be evident with able children who are concerned about being ostracized for their exceptional ability.

Rewards can be non-verbal, such as a smile or placing good work on display, or asking them to tell the rest of the class about their work in the plenary.

Rewards can also be more tangible. They can be part of a behaviourist approach to learning. Good behaviour and work is reinforced by rewards (points, praise, sharing work with a wider audience, etc.). Rewards can be used by the teacher as an overt indicator of quality work. Be sure to reward quality work rather than a large quantity of mediocre work.

NB If you have to tell someone off, it is appropriate to speak to them quietly on a one-to-one basis and always leave them with a way forward.

Links

Competition
Discipline
Motivation

Strategies

- Try to make sure all whole class comments are either positive or instructional.
- Deal with poor work/behaviour on a one-to-one basis.
- Use rewards in appropriate situations such as;
      good behaviour;
      good effort;
      a small step of improved performance;
      quality work.
- Be fair in offers of rewards.
- Do not withdraw rewards already given.

- Reward more able students and older students through written comment or one-to-one conversation if this is more appropriate.

Development

Some schools use powerful reward systems to instigate new behaviour and work patterns. One such system has younger students (Years 7–9) banking points through the week for good behaviour and work. Then the best group and individuals are rewarded with treats such as extra break time. Cumulative good responses from a register or tutor group might be rewarded with a school visit. This is a strong, behaviourist strategy to encourage change, which utilizes the desire for reward and willingness to compete.

Behaviourist research (Skinner, 1974) indicates that removal of rewards does not eliminate poor behaviour. Skinner also believed that rewards need to be frequently reinforced to establish good behaviour.

Further reading

Skinner, B. (1974) *About Behaviourism*, London: Cape.

Safety

Everyone who works in school has a *duty of care* to keep learners safe. For teachers the duty of care implies more than acting as a 'good and careful parent'. In the UK and many other countries teachers have a statutory obligation to assess risks in all types of situations. Risk assessments involving physical safety are likely to be high on most schools' agendas. You will see teachers taking care over how students are trained to behave when faced with physical danger, however slight that may be. For example, youngsters will be trained to carry scissors in such a way as to minimize danger. Beyond this, where the welfare of the student is central to the values and ethos of the school; action may be taken to address wider issues. These may include, sex education, anti-drugs education, anti-smoking education, anti-bullying policies, healthy eating education, environmental education, road safety, personal protection, education for sustainable development, or whatever is currently of general concern.

Risk assessment

A hazard means anything that can cause harm, while risk is the chance that someone might get hurt. Risks can be high or low. Your task is to make sure that the precautions you take mean that the risk is small. Getting rid of some risks is an obvious choice. But making students' lives entirely hazard free is not an option. Helping them to make the right choices about risk is part of the job. You may need to expose students to some hazards so that they can begin to make choices about risk for themselves. At the same time you need to make sure that the risks are as small as possible so as to avoid accidents. The law says that you have to take reasonable precautions.

Usually, the younger the child the higher the risk of harm. But you'll always have some students who are not very sensible about risk. You'll need to take especial care with them. Think too about the needs of students with disabilities. Looking carefully at hazards in the subjects you teach and in the space in which you work, should be a regular part of your work. Think about the groups that you teach and the degree of risk to which they should be exposed. You'll need to be especially careful when you take students away from school on visits. For out-of-school activities you will be required to complete a risk assessment form.

There are five steps in risk assessment.

1. Look for hazards.
2. Decide who might be hurt and how.
3. Evaluate the risk to decide about precautions.
4. Record your findings.
5. Review your assessment at regular intervals or at end points for one off events.

Links

Child protection
Learning environment
Out-of-school learning opportunities
Purposeful working atmosphere

Strategies

- Know what hazards are associated with the subjects you teach.
- Know how to minimize the risks in the subject.

- Agree with the students what the safety rules for movement around the teaching space and the school are.
- Teach safety rules.
- Reward students who behave safely.
- Be prepared to punish students who are frequently reckless, (see *Discipline* entry for punishment strategies).
- Know the procedures for risk assessment in your school.
- Deal with accidents promptly. Make sure that you review what happened and take appropriate action to reduce the chance of a similar incident. Keep a written note, dated and signed.

On out-of-school activities:

- Undertake a preliminary visit that includes information you'll need for risk assessment that complies with school policy.
- Write a risk assessment and have this agreed with an appropriate member of staff.
- Inform parents in writing about the benefits and possible risks in the activity; obtain written permission from them.
- Prepare students for the out-of-school activity by including discussion about health and safety rules.
- Ensure that a suitable number of adults are available, who are able to accompany and to take responsibility for students.
- Make sure that all adults who are going to be responsible for the students whilst they are out-of-school are aware of, and will apply the safety rules.
- Review the health and safety aspects of activities as part of your evaluation of the event.
- If any incidents occur, make a signed record of the sequence of events as soon as possible.

Further reading

Websites often offer the most up-to-date information on safety issues.
www.gov.uk/h_s_ev/ has general guidance on both educational visits and risk assessment as applies to England and Wales.
www.teachernet.gov.uk/visits   Sets out good practice for health and safety on visits.

TTA Standards
3.13, 3.3.8.

Self-assessment by students

In many school policies on teaching and learning, one of the aims is to enable students to become independent learners. Self-evaluation is one of the strategies which will contribute to this goal. Your students can use the process recommended in the first section of this book, just as well as adults. It is probably not appropriate to use the forms but the thinking process, as shown in the examples, is powerful. Students can ask the following questions about their work, behaviour, motivation, etc.:

> 'What do I want to improve?'
> 'What do I need to change?'
> 'What can I try out?'
> 'Did it work?'

This approach is closely aligned to the problem solving processes and cognitive acceleration strategies currently being promoted. It is a proactive approach and powerful mechanism for bringing about change.

When you ask a student to reflect on the quality of the work or behaviour he/she has produced, and he/she can respond by recognizing its worth and the need for improvement, the student has made a step towards his/her own decision making. Once students articulate what it is they are having difficulty with, they often seek help from peers and resolve the problem before it reaches the teacher.

Links

Active learning
Independent learning
Motivation
Part One
Target setting

Strategies

- Teach the steps of self-evaluation in appropriate lessons.
- Allow students the opportunity to comment on their own work or behaviour.
- Encourage verbal/written reflection and suggested action.

- Allow students to target set in specific areas (e.g. completing work, subject facts, projects, deadlines for phases of an extended piece of work).
- Introduce overt reflective discussion (possibly by showing how you carry it out through talking aloud).
- Allow students to seek peer help with problems.
- Get students to set targets and report back on them.

Development

One of the purposes of self-assessment is to reflect on what you know, but another part is to establish what you need to do. In truly proactive fashion, this will lead to target setting and further self-assessment. This would be a powerful learning tool if students too could manage the process for themselves. Pollard and Trigg (1997) suggest a three-stage strategy for establishing self-assessment with students:

1. Share aims and plan targets.
2. Review and record achievements.
3. Help report progress.

Further reading

Pollard, A. and Trigg, P. (1997) *The Reflective Teacher in the Secondary School*, London: Continuum. See Chapter 15, section 2.3.

TTA Standard

3.2.2.

Social development

Learning to be a social being is extremely important. If we want a just society then we'll see this as part of a teacher's job to make a learning environment where this can happen. Part of social development is about gaining concepts about gender, ethnicity, morality, citizenship and culture. Observing the influence of friends on the students you teach, you'll already know that peer groups have an effect on achievement. There is evidence that students need to be accepted by their peer groups in order to do well at school (see for example, Rubin and Coplan, 1992; Wentzel and Asher, 1995). Consideration for the whole person is at the centre of this. School provides a safe space, outside the home, where an understanding of society can be explored. This may be done formally through Personal, Social, Health Education (PSHE) and Citizenship teaching in tutor groups. It is about the values and ethos that underpin what the adults in the school try to do with its students, across the whole curriculum. You'll want to consider how your subject teaching can develop your students' social abilities.

Social interactions develop alongside intellectual, linguistic and physical capabilities. Erickson (1963), a developmental psychologist, gives a framework for understanding personal human development, suggesting stages that lead to self-sufficiency in adolescence. He suggests the need for a safe and secure environment to develop trust.

Briefly, the milestones in social development in Western societies are:

Babies take an interest in other babies at about 6 months; they smile and make noises at each other. By 12 months some turn-taking can be seen.

Between 12–24 months, infants play in *parallel*, that is, they play alongside each other rather than together. They start to become aware of a world beyond themselves, engaging in the rules that govern social exchange, for example, turn-taking in conversation, expressing empathy, 'Mummy sad', 'Dad cross'.

At 3 years *co-operative play* with turn-taking starts. When playing the children start to know who to give in to and how to be in charge.

4 years sees *associative play* with sharing play items. *Theory of mind*, being able to understand the position of someone else, is acquired. Fighting is a normal development happening.

By school age 6-year-olds have more friends and enemies and play in bigger groups; fights and feuds are sorted out with less adult help.

7–9-year-olds work out how to 'do friendship', what they need to be accepted as peers.

In adolescence friends become as, or more, important than parents for social support. Girls tell their best girlfriend(s) lots of things that their parents may not know. Choosing whom to associate with becomes an individual choice. Often these are same sex groupings with similarities, race, religion, similar academic and personality types. However, opposites may also attract, someone with complementary characteristics is sought. It may be that parents will not approve the choice made.

Early in teen years large groups are formed of often, but not always, boys, with a shared interest, e.g. music, football, and clothing. These groups may dare to do things that, on their own, students wouldn't attempt. The relationships within different contexts may be complex, with different groupings in different settings. As sexuality becomes important, adolescents begin to pair off. By the end of adolescence there are often couples with a smaller circle of like-minded friends.

Links

Culture
Discipline
Emotional development
Ethnicity
Intellectual development
Relationships with students

Further reading

Coleman, J. C. and Hendry, L. B. (1999) *The Nature of Adolescence*, 3rd edn, London: Routledge. Chapter 8 is useful on friendship and peer groups.

Erickson, E. H. (1963) *Childhood and Society*, New York: Norton.

Keenan, T. (2002) *An Introduction to Child Development*, London: Sage. Chapter 9 'Social development' is a useful introduction to some of the issues.

Meece, J. L. (1997) *Child and Adolescent Development for Educators*, New York: McGraw Hill. See pp. 323–6 for a succinct version of Erikson's theory.

Rubin, K. H. and Coplan, R. (1992) 'Peer relationships in childhood' in M. Bornstein and M. Lamb (Eds) *Developmental Psychology: An Advanced Textbook*, 4th edn, Mahwah, NJ: Erlbaum, pp. 451–501.

Wentzel, K. R. and Asher, S. R. (1995) 'The academic lives of neglected, rejected, popular and controversial children', *Child Development*, 66, 754–63.

TTA Standard

2.4.

Special Educational Needs

You will be meeting the needs of *all* those who you teach. Some of the students in your classes will have *barriers to learning* (a key term in inclusion). These fall into a number of categories.

1. Anybody can have an off-day or two. From time to time there will be a slight dip in the way someone behaves or in the work done. Often these are just for a very short time and you will scarcely notice them. This is not a real cause for concern.
2. Then there are students with temporary Special Educational Needs (SEN). These temporary barriers to learning may be a learning difficulty such as more than usual difficulty in reading, or spelling, or learning the facts for your subject. Other temporary special needs may be caused by distress or illness or other causes. With appropriate teaching and support the temporary needs will pass and not remain a concern.
3. Students with more permanent barriers to learning need to have their special needs addressed throughout their schooling. Many students in this category come into secondary education with their learning requirements and ways that help them learn already in place.

Meeting these needs, either those that will pass or those that don't, presents a real challenge to teachers.

The *Special Needs Co-ordinator (SENCO)* is the person to ask about the students with SEN. This is a key member of staff with specific information, resources and, most importantly, extra knowledge to help you to plan and deliver appropriate teaching, as you will be responsible for delivering your subject effectively to all students, including students with SEN.

In the classes you teach, you'll be the one to spot any student who isn't making the progress in your subject you'd expect for their age and developmental stage. Schooling makes demands on students that the home and community may not. For example, students have to be co-operative members of classes in order to learn and to stick at tasks that demand attention. Despite their previous school experience (or perhaps, because of it), you may find students in your classes who, for example, cannot do the work that others can, are really unco-operative rather than occasionally difficult, or have a very short attention span. These are examples that may mean that these students have special needs. Should you be correct in your assessment, either about academic achievement or behaviour, your concern will trigger the events that are needed for School Action. Your school will have a procedure for you to follow to get things moving. See *Code of Practice* for an explanation of the terms and procedures.

Students with an *Individual Education Plan* (IEP) in School Action or School Action Plus will be reliant on you to provide appropriate differentiated teaching for their needs in your subject. Students come into secondary education with an IEP which will identify short-term targets, which are *different* from or *additional* to those you'll set for the rest of the class. The IEP is an important tool. The targets in the IEP should be SMART:

Specific to the needs of the student
Measurable
Achievable
Realistic and
Time limited

Most schools use a simple format for IEPs. Often a software package is used to write them. The IEP should supply the information you require to help you. You will also need students' records to find out what they *can do* and what they *already know*. Use this information, with the IEP targets, to differentiate further the work you set. For example, a student who finds literacy difficult, needs small steps in learning and takes longer to understand what you are teaching, you may need to:

rewrite worksheets using short sentences and non-technical words, (even then you may need someone to read it to the students);
break tasks into small steps; give each step out one at a time;
allow extra learning time for key concepts by setting the rest of your students more complex and demanding tasks.

Take the time to differentiate the work you set and the ways in which you teach. Once you have successful tasks and materials make these reusable, rather than throw away, resources. Keep your successful teaching strategies, drop those that aren't helpful.

You will be contributing to IEPs for the students with SEN. When subject teaching, you will be making reports on students with SEN and those who may have special needs, i.e. a student whose need has just come to notice. Beyond your subject teaching, you have an important role in your register or tutor group. Your knowledge about the students in this group is very, very important. In your own group, for the students with SEN and students who are causing concern, it is likely that you will be asked to collect and make sense of the information gathered from all the subject areas to contribute to School Action and School Action Plus. You'll be contributing perhaps, to even writing their IEPs, setting targets, thinking about the way these should be taught and how to manage this, and how and when to monitor progress.

When a student in your register or tutor group has newly identified needs, often the SENCO will conduct the first interviews with him/her and the parents, alerting them to the special need and the proposed action. Your responsibility will be to help the student to understand how to make progress. As the student's form teacher or group tutor you'll certainly be helping to keep parents informed, in the reports that you write and at meetings. You'll be given support to do this.

Some students with SEN will have *learning assistants*, who are classroom assistants assigned to help them. It is still your job to differentiate your teaching, design and set the tasks to meet the learning outcomes. The learning assistant may be able to help you to do this more effectively because of their knowledge about and experience with the students. They may know about and select additional resources and generally make your learning outcomes realistic and achievable for these students. Usually the students they support have exceptionally severe and often permanent learning difficulties. These may include intellectual impairment sometimes in combination with sensory or physical impairment which may include sight, hearing and or mobility difficulties.

Some students may have sensory or physical impairments which do not impede their learning ability, and they may have a classroom assistant to help overcome the difficulty. You will be expected to take their needs into account in your teaching and to use the classroom assistant to do this. For example:

A student with a sight impairment may need a print size of 24 or even 32 point, plus a strong electric light to undertake the worksheet you are setting for the most able students in the class. The classroom assistant needs the worksheet in good time in order to prepare it.

A student with a hearing impairment may need you to use an amplifier so that your speech can be heard. The classroom assistant will check that the student can hear you.

Wheelchair users often require more space. The classroom assistant will help you organize the rest of the students to give this space.

Use any extra help you can get. Ideally, this will be an efficient and experienced learning assistant, but don't rule out volunteers. Older students working with younger students, peer support, community helpers, all are tried and tested, and, given the right set of circumstances, they work. Remember parents can often support their own child and do so willingly and well.

The need to deal effectively with students with *emotional and behavioural difficulties* (EBD) is becoming more important. These students will have IEPs with short-term targets for behaviour, sometimes referred to as an Individual Behaviour Plan (IBP). This is often in the form of an agreed contract between the student and the teachers. The contract will start with an area where you and the student think progress can be made. It will set out exactly what the student needs to do in specific contexts, for example the student is required to start on work as soon as it is set and to finish a specified amount of work each day. There may be 'time out' strategies for when the student feels that he or she may be about to lose control. For example, he or she may go, with your permission, to another class for five minutes.

On the occasions when things go seriously wrong for the student with EBD, there should be an agreed system for getting additional support into the class quickly and without fuss. You may not leave the class, so send one or two reliable students to fetch the designated teacher. The support should be from a senior member of staff: you'll need support from more experienced staff to meet some challenging behaviours. Students with severe and persistent difficulties may get extra help from a learning assistant.

The aim is always to keep focusing on achievable targets for the student. It is not the person but the acts the person carries out which are offensive and unacceptable. With your colleagues you'll be working with the student to make progress towards behaviour that is normal or near normal. You'll need to use a graduated response to students with EBD. Recognize that they may need much more positive reinforcement that other students. You always

need to have one more step in your repertoire to deal effectively with
students with EBD.

Common terms and learning difficulties

These are some of the terms you may need to know. This list is by no
means complete. Your SENCO will help you with the less common
and the more esoteric conditions that some students have. The
'health warning' is that it is not possible to generalize from the
condition, the way it will affect the individual student. Each student
experiences and overcomes difficulties in his/her own way. Whilst
your SENCO will suggest ways that often work for many students,
don't expect these to be foolproof. You and your colleagues may
have to work hard sometimes to spot what works for a particular
student. It is a great feeling when this happens.

   AD(H)D *Attention Deficit (Hyperactivity) Disorder*   Usually there
are three areas of behaviour – inattentiveness, implusivity and
overactivity – that are barriers to learning. Some of these students
need highly structured programmes to make progress in school. Each
student with ADD will have an individual pattern of behaviour with
different 'triggers' and responses dependent on a range of things –
who the teacher is, the subject, the time of day, what happened just
before your lesson, (e.g. an exciting break time), etc.

   MLD *Mild learning difficulties/moderate learning difficulties*
There are a wide range of these. Many students may have difficulty
with one or all the key skills. Some can learn well but they may
need much more time and help than others in the same class.
Others may have organizational difficulties, things like often being
late, frequently with the wrong pieces of kit, and getting lost. Many
students develop excellent coping strategies and should be expected
to develop as learners.

   SLD *Specific Learning Difficulties (including dyslexia)*   Some or
all of the following may be seen in some students: difficulty in
sequencing, difficulty with spelling, difficulty in remembering a
sequence of sounds in words, difficulty in recall of item and
number sequences, and poor handwriting. Usually, if well taught,
these students will find learning paths and develop strategies that
compensate for these barriers to learning.

   Asperger's Syndrome   This is part of the spectrum that is called
autism. Students with this can do very well in school settings with
appropriate support. In primary school they may have had delayed

speech, cognitive difficulties, problems with understanding and using social cues, an absorbing interest. Over time some of these improve, especially where help is given to the student to develop coping strategies.

Dyspraxia   Often described as clumsy, these students have difficulties in planning and carrying out skilled, non-habitual motor tasks in a correct sequence. It is sensible to allow students with dyspraxia extra time to complete tasks. They often need structured support with many motor tasks.

Links

Code of Practice
Differentiation
Inclusion
Learning styles
Monitoring and assessment strategies
Recording individual progress
Research and its uses
Teaching in teams
Working with other adults

Strategies

How would you provide proof for 'yes' answers to these questions? Turn these into statements to use as strategies or targets.

- Do I make sure that all the students in my classes take part in all lessons?
- Do I plan lessons to include all students' needs?
- Do I use different learning styles and teaching approaches? Do I for example, experiment with ways of presenting things that don't need much skill in reading?
- Do tasks and activities allow different students to get to different outcomes?
- Do I allow students with SEN the extra time they need to learn the facts and knowledge needed, by setting other students more complex and demanding tasks? (But not tasks that require new facts or knowledge otherwise students with SEN never catch up.)
- Are all students encouraged both to reflect on their own ways of learning and assess what they have learned?
- Are other adults encouraged to work with the students in my class?

- Do I make sensible use of support staff, including them in my lesson planning and preparation?
- Do we celebrate the successes we have?
- Do I enjoy the challenge that students with SEN present?

Development

Other countries have their own policies about SEN. Some segregate students with SEN into specialized schools. This is what used to happen in England and Wales. Recently though, inclusion is on the agenda for schools. Inclusion is not just about SEN, but it is true that it is far the largest area of concern for teachers, parents and policy makers. The policy was made explicit in 1997 in a DfEE consultation document *Excellence for All Children: Meeting Special Educational Needs*. This was used as an opportunity to review aspects of the education of children and young people with learning and other barriers to success. The key principles of early identification and appropriate intervention were made policy. It was a major review of principles established by the Warnock Report (DES, 1978) and included a revision of the Code of Practice (DfES, 2001a). The policy means that the number of children with SEN to be included in main stream schooling is likely to increase. See the entries on *Code of Practice* and on *Inclusion* to gain an overview on the policy and practice.

Students with SEN are often a cause of anxiety for teachers. They worry about their ability to meet the needs of *all* the students they teach and how they will cope with the extra demand made by students with SEN. Fortunately, there is a wealth of information and experience on how to do this. In school, the SENCO can often help you to manage the teaching and learning so that students with SEN are not a burden. There are excellent books, websites and courses for teachers. What is true is that students with SEN are often key in making each of us more effective teachers for all our students. They are the students who teach us how to teach. Meeting their special needs makes us think hard about teaching and learning. This makes us more aware of how we might teach concepts, facts, skills, knowledge, ideas and values to *all* our students, not just students with SEN. You may find that students with SEN are particularly rewarding to teach. If this is the case then developing this aspect of your career is something you should consider.

Further reading

There are a great many books and websites and organizations with useful information on SEN as a whole and on most of the conditions associated with particular special needs. The following is a short list:

Benton, P. and O'Brien, T. (Eds) (2000) *Special Needs and the Beginning Teacher*, London: Continuum.

Carpenter, B., Ashdown, R. and Bovair, K. (Eds) (2001) *Enabling Access: Effective Learning for Pupils with Learning Difficulties*, 2nd edn, London: David Fulton.

Department for Education and Employment (DfEE) (1997) *Excellence for all Children, Meeting Special Educational Needs*, London: DfEE.

Department of Education and Science (DES) (1978) *Report on the Commission on Special Education*, London: HMSO (Warnock Report).

Department for Education and Skills (DfES) (2001a) *Special Needs Code of Practice* (DfES 581/2001) London DfES.

Department for Education and Skills (DfES) (2001b) *Schools Achieving Success*, London: HMSO.

Farrell, M. (2000) *The Special Education Handbook*, 2nd edn, London: David Fulton.

Flavell, E. (2001) *Preparing to Include Special Children in Mainstream Schools, A Practical Guide*, London, David Fulton.

Garner, P. and Dwyfor Davies, J. (2001) *Introducing Special Educational Needs: A Companion Guide for Student Teachers*, London: David Fulton.

Wearmouth, J. (ed.) (2001) *Special Educational Provision in the Context of Inclusion: Policy and Practice in Schools*, London: David Fulton/Open University.

Websites (Note that there are many more than these.)

See DfES webpages for the most up-to-date information about SEN and Connexions. http://inclusion.ngfl.gov.uk and www.connexions.gov.uk

www.halcyon.com/marcs/sped.html   North American site with many useful links.

www.ipsea.org.uk   Independent advice for parents.

www.nasen.org.uk   National Association of Special Educational Needs; good links to other sites.

TTA Standards

2.6, 3.2.4, 3.3.4.

Standardized tests

These are tests which have been trialled and matched to a norm. Like IQ (Intelligence Quotient) the norm is 100; results are converted using a table. The table allows for the age of the candidate to be taken into account. The candidate does the test which is marked and a 'raw' score is generated. This is then 'converted' using a table to a 'standardized score'. If a younger candidate gains the same raw score as an older candidate, the younger candidate will get a higher standardized score. When scores or ages lie on the limits of the normal range, the test is considered to be a less reliable predictor of ability. Standardized tests can be used to compare groups in various locations as well as measuring the candidate against the norm in different years.

Links

Research and its uses
Summative assessment

Development

A standardized test can be useful in research because it gives a norm which can be used to establish a base line and then candidates can be re-tested with the knowledge that a similar test will give comparable results.

However, Croll (1996) offers a nice comparison between norm referenced and the criterion referenced assessments which have come into more common use for measuring children's performance. He indicates that it may not be easy to operate a pure criterion referenced system when we have age-related expectations. Certainly, in the light of his comments, it is worth reflecting on how a criterion referenced system is actually used in the National Curriculum (DfEE, 2000).

Further reading

Croll, P. (1996) 'Norm and criterion referenced assessment' in Pollard, A.
    (Ed.) *Readings for Reflective Teaching in the Primary School*, London:
    Continuum.
Department for Education and Employment (DfEE) (2000) *The National
    Curriculum: Handbook for Primary Teachers in England Key Stages 1
    and 2*, London: DfEE/QCA (www.nc.uk.net).
Pollard, A. and Trigg, P. (1997) *The Reflective Teacher in the Secondary
    School*, London: Continuum.
www.nc.gov.uk
www.qca.uk/ca/tests

TTA Standard

3.2.3.

Subject knowledge

In teaching you need a good knowledge of the subjects you are going to teach plus a knowledge of how to teach them (pedagogic knowledge). For example, knowing how to do a long multiplication sum is not enough. Can you explain clearly to learners how to do long multiplication and why it works? Do you have other methods students could use if they cannot grasp the first method? As a teacher there is a significant shift to be made from having personal knowledge to having words to successfully teach that knowledge and finding tasks to help students understand that knowledge.

If you are confident and knowledgeable about your subject you will provide correct information to students and you will be able to answer their questions. You will also convey a sense of structure and continuity in the work that you do with them. You will be in a better position to challenge students' thinking and will be able to resolve their misconceptions. Enthusiasm for your subject is easily conveyed to students. Unfortunately the opposite can be true too.

There are some aspects of your subjects which will be your strengths and those you teach will benefit from your expertise. In the topics where you are not so knowledgeable you will need to research and prepare your medium- and short-term planning carefully. Within a department, or faculty staff you will often be able to find someone who will be able to provide some support with your weaker topic areas.

Links

Active learning
Independent learning
Medium-term planning
Research and its uses

Strategies

- Research areas you are not sure of so that you provide an accurate and true experience for the student.
- Convey enthusiasm.
- Seek guidance when you need it.
- Inform yourself well on topics as you teach them.
- Find opportunities, such as courses and conferences, to strengthen your knowledge and teaching.

Development

A depth of subject knowledge and a particular interest in a subject will enhance your teaching and will often prove a strong motivator for the students. Spontaneous questions will elicit knowledgeable responses from you. You may even provide additional and interesting explanations which you, from your knowledge base, see as connected information, things which another teacher will be unaware of. This allows you to extend students' thinking and is particularly stimulating for able students.

Teachers who have a good knowledge base in a subject are more likely to be relaxed about teaching the subject, enthusiastic about the subject and less likely to teach misconceptions.

Further reading

For further information on subject and other requirements see www.nc.gov.uk and www.canteach.gov.uk.

TTA Standard

2.1.

Summative assessment

Summative assessments are those that are made to summarize performance. They tend to mark stages of progress through the education system. The main purpose of summative assessment is to identify the stage a student has reached at that point in time. Where marked papers are returned, these can be used for formative assessment. English national tests' results are analysed and the results are sent to schools to inform them about weaknesses in particular topics. Analysis of individual papers can indicate a student's individual areas of difficulty. In England, typical summative assessments are GCSE exams, key stage tests and GNVQ. The key stage tests are analysed and a report provided on national performance, which means that summative assessment can be used in a formative way.

Within school, summative assessment might take the form of half-termly and end-of-year tests, end of topic assessments, end of year records to pass on to other teachers, reports to parents, or records of achievement.

Links

Formative assessment
National qualifications
Recording individual progress

Strategies

- Ensure ongoing records are kept which will inform you when you need to summarize a student's achievements.
- Provide an assessment to summarize what a student understands about a subject at this point in time.
- Consider the use of self-evaluation when judging what a student does/does not know.
- Be familiar with national assessment requirements.

Development

Assessment is used for many different purposes and therefore it is important that you select a form of assessment which provides you with the information you need. For a good summary of the purposes and principles of assessment refer to Harlen *et al.* (1996) p. 264. Don't be put off by the word 'primary' as the reading has universal application!

Further reading

Harlen, W., Gipps, C., Broadfoot, P. and Nuttall, D. (1996) 'Assessment purposes and principles' in Pollard, A. (Ed.) *Readings for Reflective Teaching in the Primary School*, London: Continuum.
www.nc.gov.uk
www.qca.org.uk

TTA Standards

3.2.2, 3.2.3.

Target setting

The purpose of target setting is to have clear goals which focus learning. There are several layers of target setting occurring in school. The teacher will have targets for whole class learning and for individuals (learning objectives). Target setting for students could be part of a pupil self-evaluation system. Some target setting for students is shared with parents. It is particularly important that achievement of these targets is recognized. This can be difficult to organize at the end of the school year.

Target setting for the teacher is part of your self-evaluation system and continuing professional development. A more formal target setting for teachers can be met when participating in an appraisal system. Here the targets are usually set for a whole year.

In England schools have targets too. These are shown in the School Improvement Plan. Many LEAs set schools targets to achieve in key stage tests. These are usually projections of baseline assessment or previous Key Stage results. These targets are part of the drive to raise standards in schools throughout England. Inspections can result in actionable comments which then become school targets in the development plan.

Links

Active learning
Continuing professional development
Monitoring students' learning
Summative assessment
Teachers' employment and conditions

Strategies

- Set clear objectives in long-, medium- and short-term planning and monitor students' achievement of them.
- Create time to set targets with individuals and time to follow them up.
- Encourage students to evaluate what they have done and what they need to do next.
- Be aware of national and local target setting for your school. Match these to your subject performance indicators.
- Set targets for yourself about your teaching skills.

Development

Individualized target setting systems are time consuming to maintain. However, they are an effective way of meeting the needs of individual students. With individual targets it is worth getting the co-operation of the student in setting the target, as much of the work will take place in the student's own time. They will also need to know how they can go about achieving the target. A well-known acronym for target setting is SMART which stands for, **S**pecific, **M**easurable, **A**greed, **R**ealistic, **T**ime limited, all qualities which good target setting should include.

Smith (2001) describes a process for successfully establishing target setting. His five steps are; time lines, future-basing, templates, anchoring and affirmations.

A fundamental issue when running a target setting system is to establish how you will monitor that the targets have been achieved. This needs planning in to your medium- and short-term strategies. No matter how independently a student is able to work, you are part of the contract which is made when the target is set. If you do not follow up the target setting the motivation will die and the system become non-effective.

Further reading

Smith, A. (2001) 'The strategies to accelerate learning in the classroom' in Banks, F. and Shelton Mayes, A. (Eds) *Early Professional Development for Teachers*, London: David Fulton/Open University, p. 168–71.

TTA Standard

3.1.

Teachers' employment and conditions

In England and Wales these are reviewed annually. The pay structure is fixed by law. However, whilst there is some automatic annual progression increasingly your employers, the governors, have scope for discretion. The school will have a policy document about pay and conditions. Your job description will say what your school expects from you, and should be reviewed and updated regularly. It will state both the generic roles you'll be expected to undertake and any specific tasks that are your responsibility. In England teachers work 195 days a year, five of these are training days. Hours are also specified, but there is a let-out phrase on this, as you have to discharge effectively your professional duties. This means that most teachers work much more than a 36-hour week. Professional duties include teaching, preparation for teaching, marking and report writing. Your workload is determined by the headteacher or your line manager, who is probably your subject department or faculty leader.

Performance management means that you will continue to be a life-long learner. You will be developing the professional portfolio you started pre qualification. As a newly qualified teacher (NQT) you'll start your first post with some targets. As there is always something more to understand as a teacher, targets will not be hard to find. Furthermore, in most education systems, the extra experience gained will boost income. This aspect of your career is managed over a two-year cycle.

Your work is under scrutiny all the time. At first this is intimidating but you will soon become used to it. The results you get and how you teach will be inspected regularly. These judgements will be used in different ways, one of which is to plan for your development. In addition to the appraisal you get from your colleagues, there are local inspectors and the Office for Standards in Education (Ofsted) inspectors, who are in schools as part of the local and national accountability and quality system for England. Judgements made about your work contribute to the judgement made about the school.

Links

Continuing professional development (CPD)
Learning environment
Values and ethos

Strategies

- Be ambitious about all those you teach – expect them to do well and to achieve.
- Be aware of the expectations your colleagues have about you, know what your professional responsibilities are and undertake these wholeheartedly (see *Development* below).
- Before accepting employment check that the pay and conditions are what you want, including arrangements for your support and further opportunities for Continuing Professional Development.
- Prepare thoroughly for all aspects of performance review.
- Set realistic targets for your own development, these should take account of those the school has as its focus.
- Choose CPD activities that can be used to develop your curriculum vitae (CV).

Development

Beyond pay and conditions you'll want to understand what teaching involves. An important part of your professional responsibilities is the expectations you have about those who you teach. As a teacher you are expected to want your students to do as well as they possibly can. This means that you won't accept anything less than the best from everyone. Their 'best' means working towards raising achievement in all aspects of learning. But it also means that you have to do this from a knowledge base that respects and deals with difference. How you treat your students and work with colleagues, support workers, parents and all those you come into contact with through your work, will demonstrate your understanding of your responsibilities. You are expected to evaluate yourself as a teacher, to build on your strengths and to improve on any weaknesses. You'll work within the rules that are laid down by statute. This is a great deal to take on. It doesn't all have to be learned at once but it does all have to be learned.

Further reading

Cowley, S. (1999) *Starting Teaching: How to Succeed and Survive*, London: Continuum. Part IV is about teachers' employment.

Dillon, J. and Maguire, M. (Eds) (2001) *Becoming a Teacher: Issues in Secondary Teaching*, 2nd edn, Buckingham: Open University Press. Chapter 11, by Dylan William, on 'Teachers and the law', adds another dimension to this as an issue.

www.canteach.gov.uk has useful links.

www.teachernet.gov.uk has the most up-to-date information about employment for teachers in England.

TTA Standard

1.8.

Teaching in teams

You are responsible for working with your teacher colleagues, who will expect you to share responsibility for the school curriculum in all sorts of ways. They will expect a professional commitment to joint planning and preparation. You will need help to overcome some of the barriers to learning that some of the students in your class may have. Other students are very able so ask for help with getting the targets and work right for them. Colleagues will expect you to be willing to work towards solutions to challenges, particularly in your subject. You will have responsibilities for the welfare of the students in your classes. You will be expected to report on anything you think is amiss, as well as celebrating students' successes. You will need to know about the students in your register or tutor group. Other teachers will require information about them from you. You'll be involved in helping to make decisions about and with students from this group. You will be aware of the issues that face the school as a whole. The management group of more senior teachers will expect your support and understanding.

Links

Continuing professional development (CPD)
Teachers' employment and conditions
Working with other adults

Strategies

As a colleague:

- Know your personal qualities, work from your strengths, but address your weaknesses.
- Be prepared to be flexible; it's supportive to release a classroom assistant on occasions to help in another class, it's a help to take a few extra students sometimes, it's ok to change your mind when there is new information.
- Empathy – putting yourself in someone else's position, understanding not just the words but the emotions that are underneath – is a real strength. In the staff room, at your subject meetings, listen to what is meant not just what is said.
- Be task involved. Judge yourself and others on what is done not by who does it. It is about doing your best and doing an honest job.
- Be assertive. For example, accept thanks graciously, find a form of words to tell someone why you are annoyed, 'When you do ... I find there is a problem. Can we find a way to deal with this?'.
- Keep a hold on your sense of humour. There are times when humour can really help. But not always!
- Develop your understanding of the structures within which your school works, how it is governed, the challenges and the plan that has been agreed with the governors to meet these.

- Attend meetings and read the notes that are sent round and e-mails (even when these seem, at first, to make little sense.)
- Listen, ask questions, take part in the staffroom banter and conversations. It is tempting to stay in your own area when you have a great deal to do, but if you want to really be a part of the school, get into the staffroom, get yourself known and get to know colleagues. Beware though, of the staffroom cynics, often they are very attractive company, witty and sharp, but their comments can lower morale.

Development

Being part of a team means that you will get support in your day to day work and in career planning. Your colleagues will suggest when you should take on additional responsibility. Fairly soon, perhaps in your second year as a teacher, you will want to think about this. A particular project, within your subject department, is often the first move. Think too about a wider role, working with parents and volunteers or being the teacher representative on the Governing Body or moving into union or professional association work. Moving school to gain experience with a different team is another decision that you will want to make at some point.

Further reading

Cowley, S. (1999) *Starting Teaching: How to Succeed and Survive*, London: Continuum.

Thody, A., Gray, B. and Bowden, D. (2000) *The Teacher's Survival Guide*, London: Continuum.

TTA Standards

1.5, 1.6, 3.1.4, 3.3.13.

Thinking skills (including cognitive acceleration)

As technology develops the needs of society are changing and access to information is easier. This has brought about a subtle change in education. The need now is to educate people to manage the new technologies, to be able to solve problems and make decisions. This has tipped the balance of skills and knowledge slightly more in the direction of skills, particularly problem solving and thinking skills. Also, in the effort to raise standards of pupil achievement in education people are examining the ways in which students learn effectively, hoping this will unlock the door to learning. Research into thinking and cognitive acceleration is currently being utilized to create better learning environments for students. What is particularly exciting is that this work, once the domain of psychologists, is now being linked to practical classroom strategies with interesting results (CASE, 1988, Adhami *et al.*, 1997, Smith, 2001).

Links

Able students
Active learning
Independent learning
Problem solving
Learning styles
Questioning
Target setting

Strategies

- Discuss with students how they will go about a task.
- Promote problem solving strategies.
- Get students to set targets.
- Make sure students are aware and understand the learning objective and how it is to be achieved.
- Get students to reflect on the mental strategies that they are using.
- Encourage articulation of how they are working things out.

Development

Reflecting on the way we think ourselves is often termed metacognition. Thinking skills have long been a subject for study but two recent research projects at King's College, London University are generating much interest. These are *Cognitive Acceleration in Science Education* (CASE) (Adey, 1988) and *Cognitive Acceleration in Mathematics Education* (CAME) (Adhami *et al.*, 1997). Cognitive acceleration is a term used to describe a process which allows students to speed up their ability to learn. By teaching students to understand the way they work and to develop strategies for solving problems, it is believed students can learn more effectively and perform to a higher level. Results from both CASE and CAME, which are based on Piagetian problem solving, have been very promising in showing improvement and are transfering to other subjects. Other projects where students employ metacognitive techniques are also currently popular. These techniques require the student to consciously consider what processes and strategies they are using when working at a task. Smith (2001) discusses 'pole-bridging' which is about utilizing as much of the brain as possible when doing a task. This can be done by articulating aloud what you are doing as you do it (talk yourself through, take notes, reflect and hypothesize on the situation). The plenary of a lesson often involves a form of reflection on the lesson. Smith goes on to discuss recent research on how our brains work and how we can maximize the learning environment of the classroom by utilizing this knowledge.

Further reading

Smith, A. (2001) 'What the most recent brain research tells us about learning' in Banks, F. and Shelton Mayes, A. (Eds) *Early Professional Development for Teachers*, London: David Fulton/Open University.

Adey, P. (1988) 'Cognitive acceleration: review and prospects' in *International Journal of Science Education*, 10, 2, 121–34.

Adhami, M., Johnson, D. and Shayer, M. (1997) 'Does "CAME" work? Summary report on Phase 2 of the Cognitive Acceleration in Mathematics Education, CAME, Project' in *Proceedings of the Day Conference of the British Society for Research into Learning Mathematics*, Bristol, November.

Sousa, D. A. (2001) *How the Brain Learns*, 2nd edn, Thousand Oaks: Corwin.

TTA Standard

3.2.5.

Time management

Teaching is a demanding profession so it is very important that you manage your time well and as efficiently as possible. Not only do you need good time management for yourself but you also need to expect it from your students. As a teacher, it is very easy to take on more than you can possibly manage. It is better to give a polite but firm refusal when approached, than agree and then not have time to do the job well. Work out your limitations and stick to them. This is good time management and avoids you and everyone else getting stressed. On the same theme, it is important to create your own free space, away from school work. This should be a point in the evening when you stop work and a regular commitment to a leisure time activity.

One of the classic ways to manage time effectively is to get started promptly and to limit the time to achieve tasks. If, on the other hand, you give yourself an open-ended schedule you will probably use up all of your time.

Try to avoid duplication when writing planning documents. Use key words and bullet points in your planning. Plan ahead as much as possible so that you can have part of each day to yourself. Use previous plans and ideas from text books if they are appropriate. ICT systems are useful here. Try to be efficient in your record keeping too. Decide for what purposes you need to keep records and then select the relevant information. Have a system which culminates in useful information at the end of the year.

Much of the above applies to organizing the students in your class. They too need to learn good time management habits, such as getting started promptly on tasks and knowing how long they have to expected completion. Make these expectations overt so that they learn to develop their work habits. Allow students to make judgements about work. For example, 'How long do you think you need to complete this?' and, 'How are you going to start this problem?'. Younger students also appreciate reward for work well done and well managed. This might be stars, house points, treats, etc.

Links

Completed work
Expectations about students' learning
Independent learning
Long-term planning
Medium-term planning
Rewards
Teaching in teams
Working with other adults

Strategies

- Make overt references to starting and completing work (expectations).
- Plan as far ahead as possible.

- Allow personal space in each day.
- Reward yourself and students for work well managed.

Development

Pollard and Trigg (1995) suggest ways of monitoring how students spend their time in your lessons. As there is a relationship between time on task and the learning accomplished, it is worth recording and reflecting on this from time to time.

Further reading

Capel, S. (2001) 'Unit 1.1 Managing your time and preventing stress' in Capel, S., Leask, M. and Turner, T. (Eds) *Learning to Teach in Secondary Schools*, London: Routledge. This chapter has some excellent practical advice.

Pollard, A and Trigg, P. (1997) *The Reflective Teacher in the Secondary School*, London: Continuum. See Chapters 11 and 12.

TTA Standard

3.3.7.

Timing within lessons

Timing of a lesson is a blend of planning the right length tasks, teaching within your allotted time slot, having a sense of time passing during the lesson and switching or staying with tasks depending on whether the students are engaged in a task or not.

If you check the clock at regular intervals you will build up an awareness of the time passing. At the end of the lesson you can evaluate whether you remained on schedule or not. This depends on you estimating and writing on your lesson plan how much time you anticipate using for each part of the lesson. You will begin to refine your medium-term planning to match the pace of the students you are teaching. Increasingly you will find that you are able to judge how long tasks will take and the level of the work that engages the students.

Do not be afraid to alter the timing of a lesson if things are going well or badly. It is best to move on if the students are restless and finding it difficult to pay attention. It is also your decision to extend a piece of work if you think the students are having a meaningful learning experience.

Regularly running out of time alters the balance of the lesson and means the conclusion is neglected. This is a valuable part of the lesson which gives you an opportunity to re-focus students' attention on the learning objective(s). You also need to maintain a balance between listening and doing. Overly long introductions leave little time for students to practise and consolidate the ideas and thus remember them.

Links

Lesson plan structure
Pace
Time management

Strategies

• Review timing of tasks and adapt medium- and short-term planning.
• Enter anticipated length of teaching and tasks on your lesson plan.
• Ensure that all sections of a lesson are delivered.
• Consider the balance within the lesson between listening, responding and doing tasks.

Further Reading

Pollard, A. and Trigg, P. (1997) *The Reflective Teacher in the Secondary School*, London: Continuum. See Chapters 11 and 12.

TTA Standard

3.3.7.

Transitions

Any movement from one activity to the next is called a transition. This could be when the whole class are required to enter or leave the room, when they move from whole class teaching to work individually or in groups and when they complete one task and move on to another. All these situations have the potential for some students to behave poorly and not engage in the next task. You need to be well organized, clear in your expectations and clear in your instructions so that the students have no doubt what is expected of them. If they know what they are supposed to be doing this makes it easier to deal with situations where they are not following instructions, because they clearly know they are in the wrong. Some classes and individual students will vary in their ability to make transitions with control. Ultimately you are aiming for an environment where students can move round your teaching space and from lesson to lesson in an orderly and purposeful manner without you 'policing the traffic'. This form of self-discipline needs to be encouraged and praised and opportunities offered for it to occur. In the beginning though, there might be a need to establish firm discipline and clear rules of transition.

When clearing away have a specific location for students to go when finished. You may need to do more than this. For example, it is not enough to say 'go back to your place when you have cleared away your things'. This clearing up could spread over a long period of time and the early finishers will get bored if there is nothing to do. Make sure they have a short extension or ongoing task.

Links
Discipline
Timing within lessons

Strategies
- Ensure that students enter and leave the room in an orderly fashion.
- Make your expectations clear about where students should be at the start and finish of a task before allowing them to move away from the previous situation.
- Whenever you can, make sure resources are laid out or available prior to the lesson.
- Plan extension tasks for the fast finishers.
- If students are going to finish at different times make sure they know what they are to do as and when they finish.
- Be prepared to start another activity which late finishers can join in when they complete their last task.
- If the class cannot move properly all at once send them to tasks a few at a time.

Development
Initially, managing transitions is about you having control of the class and creating an orderly environment, but it should develop from

there into a situation where students want their workspaces and school to have an atmosphere where they move around like purposeful adults and engage in tasks because they are meaningful. It should not be a place where they have to keep one eye on the teacher to see if he/she is watching them and feel they have to misbehave because the teacher's attention is elsewhere. You will be working towards discipline and then self-discipline. You should be able to move towards this by giving the students who are capable, more opportunities to manage their work. On occasions peer pressure can be used in group tasks to get the students with less self-discipline to toe the line. All the books listed below offer clear guidance on establishing your authority and increasing students' self-discipline.

Further reading

Petty, G. (1993) *Teaching Today: A Practical Guide*, Cheltenham: Stanley Thornes. Chapter 8, 'Classroom management', is a really useful guide.
Watkins, C. and Wagner, P. (2000) *Improving School Behaviour*, London: Paul Chapman. Chapter 3, 'Improving classroom behaviour', covers the same ground.
See the further reading recommended under the entry on *Discipline*.

Values and ethos

Your values will reflect in your professional role. You'll want all those you teach to succeed at the highest level. To do this you have to know and understand about yourself, those who you teach and the education system. This is a tall order, so start by examining your own values. What do you hold dear? How does this square with what the society in which you live expects from you? For example, if you think honesty is important how does this match with society's expectations? Being honest is not absolute; in part it is about knowing when to tell the truth and when it is right to keep silent. Moral judgements are not always easy to make, sometimes you just have to hope that you're doing the 'right thing'. What you do and say, in any given situation, will establish your values with the students. For example, a student who disrupts a lesson by throwing pens and pencils on the floor might be punished, but a student whose pens and pencils fall to the floor by accident would not. The distinctive atmosphere of justice and equity you establish will be recognized as your values in action and the ethos in your classes.

Links

Bullying
Culture
Discipline
Emotional development
Equal opportunities
Ethnicity
Parents
Social development
Relationships with students
Teachers' employment and conditions

Strategies

Some principles to support the strategies you use:

- Accept that you need to develop your students' sense about right and wrong (moral development).
- Know the range of social and emotional development that you're likely to meet with your students.
- Respect differences of culture in families and society.
- Recognize and deal with the fact that some students have a different view of right and wrong to your own.
- Be clear with yourself about what is acceptable behaviour and what is unacceptable in your classes.

In your relationships with students:

- Expect high standards of behaviour and work from everyone.
- Work systematically with them towards a shared idea about what this means (ethos), e.g. through discussion as a class, in pairs and group, to arrive at definitions and examples of these in action.
- Recognize that being fair does not mean treating everyone exactly the same.
- Being approachable does not mean that the learners are your friends.
- Being firm means being just in your dealings and recognizing that not everyone starts from the same place.
- Rewards and punishments may not be the same for all students.

Development

The moral, emotional and social development of learners needs to inform the decisions you make about the values you teach and the ethos you establish with your classes. The aim is always to be stretching the students' abilities to make the right choices both for them and for the society in which they live. There is a tension here. You'll want to develop a climate in which it is right to challenge the opinions of others, where acceptance of difference is normal and where ideas about social justice can be explored. This line of a strong but tolerant morality is not easy to establish. Your reputation with students for being fair has to be carefully built. Students expect you to be 'in charge' but they also expect you to respect and value their views and opinions, especially where these are at variance from accepted social norms. You'll want to be aware of the developmental range of your students, some start with a greater awareness of moral issues and dilemmas than others.

If you teach in England it is likely that you'll have responsibility for a particular group of students. Often this will involve you in teaching about values. One subject that you will need to research is citizenship.

Further reading

Arthur, J. and Wright, D. (2001) *Teaching Citizenship in the Secondary School*, London: David Fulton.

Cribb, A. and Gerwitz, S. (2001) 'Values and schooling' in Dillon, J. and Maguire, M. (Eds) *Becoming a Teacher: Issues in Secondary Teaching*, 2nd edn, Buckingham: Open University Press, pp. 37–49.

Haydon, G. (1997) *Teaching About Values: A New Approach*, London: Cassell.

Mosely, J. and Tew, M. (1999) *Quality Circle Time in the Secondary School*, London: David Fulton. This is full of useful ideas that will help you teach about values and establish the ethos you want.

TTA Standards

1.3, 3.3.1.

Whole class teaching

The Hay McBer (2000: 1.2.7) report confirms that, 'what we saw effective teachers doing was a great deal of direct instruction to whole classes, interspersed with individual and small group work'.

They comment on the high level of interaction between students and teacher. Whole class teaching has to involve all the students in the class. Everyone has to be engaged. A wide ability range may test the teacher's ability to do this. Recognize that some students take much longer to learn. You'll want to have some tasks that everyone does and something to challenge quick finishers.

Links

Demonstration by the teacher
Discipline
Explaining
Independent learning
Timing within lessons
Transitions

Strategies

In whole class teaching.

- Use a variety of methods during whole class teaching.
- Teaching and learning activities must match learning outcomes.
- Use clear instructions, demonstrations, explanations and careful questioning.
- During the lesson find out what students know and understand.
- Use carefully chosen examples, case studies and other activities that allow students to explore their learning.
- Set quick finishers more complex tasks, but not tasks that involve 'new' knowledge or understanding, i.e. the difficulty has to be in the complexity.

Development

Whole class teaching only works if the relationships between you and those you teach is interactive. The interactions between you and the students have to be based on respect and trust. Whole class teaching is at its best when learners are challenged to use higher order thinking. You'll want to use open ended questions, asking students to explain their answers, relating your questions to their ability. You'll also want to keep your teaching fresh. For example, whilst much of the whole class teaching you do may follow a similar pattern, from time to time surprise your classes with a different format.

Further reading

Hay McBer (2000) *Research into Teacher Effectiveness: A Model of Teacher Effectiveness*, London: DfEE, weblink www.dfes.gov.uk/teachingreforms/leadership/mcber/

Muijs, D. and Reynolds, D. (2001) *Effective Teaching: Evidence and Practice*, London: Paul Chapman.

TTA Standard

3.1.1.

Working with other adults

Time was when a teacher went into a classroom, closed the door and got on with teaching. These days you can expect to share the responsibility for students' progress with other adults for at least some of the time. You'll regularly work with learning assistants (or classroom assistants) and, in many subjects, with technical staff. You'll have contact with lunchtime supervisors, janitors, cleaners, maintenance workers and school office staff.

Learning assistants and technicians will expect you to know what it is you want them to do. They will also expect you to respect their expertise. It is becoming much more usual for them to have opportunities to gain qualifications and for there to be a career structure.

The learning assistant should be your best ally. The relationship you have is going to be important to both of you. Some are there to support a particular student. Others are there to help you to work effectively with all the students by, for example, supporting reading and writing. They will have a different understanding about the students from yours. Their views can add to your knowledge and inform the decisions you make. Some areas of your work are confidential. It is important to recognize that this can conflict with the open relationship you'll want to have with co-workers. Plan your teaching to make best use of the help available. They need to be involved all the time to make best use of teaching time. In particular, what is their role when you are explaining something to the whole class or managing a question and answer session? This is something to consult them about.

If your subject involves technical support you will want this to work well. Establishing a sound working relationship which gets you the support you need, given willingly by your technician, is worth some effort from you. Respecting their knowledge and expertise, asking advice, giving enough notice and accepting that you may have to modify your planning are all really important. Be precise in your requirements. Give positive feedback on the task, dealing with any difficulties that may occur promptly.

Links

Teachers' employment and conditions
Teaching in teams

Strategies

As a colleague with support workers:

- Be clear about what you want your co-worker to do to support your teaching. Make sure you make good use of their time. Share planning and write down the tasks to be done. Give learning assistants the materials for the tasks you set. Ask for feedback, and remember to say, 'thank-you'.
- Agree on the class routines and procedures, make sure that you all discipline students in similar ways.
- Involve any co-workers in problem solving and decision making. Together analyse situations, think about possible solutions, decide on actions and evaluate them. Deal with difficulties as they occur.
- Recognize and respect their expertise and knowledge.

Development

Who else is in school? There are also support roles from other agencies, social workers, educational psychologists, specialist teachers, nurses, doctors, dentists, examination invigilators, school bus drivers, cooks, the police, the list goes on and on. Many schools have volunteer helpers, parents and people from local firms and sports teams. All these people add an extra dimension to your work.

Although writing about primary schools Thomas (1989) identifies the issues for adults and students. Extra adults in class do, possibly create problems. Role ambiguity, 'who is the teacher?', may be a problem for some, including the students. Obstructing each other or duplicating tasks unintentionally is something to be avoided. Clear job specifications, ways of working and conflict resolution strategies need to be in place to make best use of additional adults.

The students need to know who does what. In class thinking about the talents that all the additional adults have and using these to best advantage is clearly important.

Further reading

Bradley, C. and Roaf, C. B. (2000) 'Working effectively with learning support assistants' in Benton, P. and O'Brien, T. (Eds) *Special Needs and the Beginning Teacher*, London: Continuum, pp. 171–91. The focus on Special Needs Support is a useful introduction to thinking about how to work with all co-workers.

O'Brien, T. and Guiney, D. (2001) *Differentiation in Teaching and Learning, Principles and Practice*, London: Continuum.

Thody, A, Gray, B. and Bowden, D. (2000) *The Teacher's Survival Guide*, London: Continuum.

Thomas, G. (1989) 'The teacher and others in the classroom' in Cullingford, C. (Ed.) *The Primary Teacher: The Role of the Educator and the Purpose of Primary Education*, London: Cassell, pp. 59–70.

TTA Standards

1.6, 3.1.4, 3.3.13.